THE *Illustrated* BOOK OF
SACRED
SCRIPTURES

TIMOTHY FREKE

D0126449

A publication supported by
THE KERN FOUNDATION

Quest Books
Theosophical Publishing House
Wheaton, Illinois ◆ Chennai (Madras), India

*This book is dedicated
to my father
who taught me that
God is Love
and my mother
who showed me that
Love is Natural*

Copyright © 1998 Godsfield Press

Text © 1998 Timothy Freke

1 2 3 4 5 6 7 8 9 10

First Quest Edition 1998
Co-published with
Godsfield Press 1998

For additional information write to

The Theosophical Publishing House
P.O. Box 270
Wheaton, IL 60189-0270

A publication of the Theosophical Publishing
House, a department of the Theosophical
Society in America

Picture research by Vanessa Fletcher

Designed by Ron Bryant-Funnell

Library of Congress Cataloging-in-Publication Data

Freke, Timothy
    The illustrated book of Sacred Scriptures / Timothy Freke.
        p. cm.
    Includes bibliographical references.
    ISBN 0-8356-0758-5
    1. Sacred books. I.Title.
BL70.F68   1997
291.8'2—dc21   97-20079
                                      CIP

Printed and bound in Singapore

THE ILLUSTRATED BOOK OF SACRED SCRIPTURES

Contents

Introduction

THE SCRIPTURES OF THE WORLD are among humanity's greatest literary riches. They have endured the test of time and the scrutiny of millions of readers, remaining a source of wisdom and inspiration for generations. Just as religious architecture has survived the rigors of the ages, so too the sacred writings of the world are a most ancient bequest from our ancestors. Sacred scriptures are among the most read and most frequently translated writings in human history.

The search for meaning and wisdom is perennial, and the insights of the scriptures are as profound and relevant today as they were for our forebears. We too have been born into a world without an instruction manual and face the challenge of living well and facing death. Although human culture changes continually, the essential mysteries inherent in the human predicament remain the same.

More than anything else, scripture exists to give us insight into these universal enigmas. This book draws on those sacred writings which have a universal, spiritual quality, allowing them to speak across the boundaries of time, place, and tradition, to address the unchanging questions of life.

In this multicultural age we are beginning to see beyond the limited horizons of our national and religious boundaries and glimpse our shared humanity. From this perspective, the scriptures of the world do not belong to this or that religion but are a common spiritual resource to inspire and illuminate all those who turn to them. Although it could be argued that particular scriptures can be understood fully only within the context of their tradition, it is not the aim of this book to elucidate various religious doctrines, but rather to let great sacred texts from all traditions inform and augment each other, creating a general overview of human spirituality.

ONE TRUTH, MANY NAMES

Nearly every religious tradition contains both those who view scripture from a fundamentalist perspective and those who view it from a mystical perspective. For fundamentalists, scripture is an indisputable testimony of the truth. Despite the internal contradictions the scriptures of every tradition contain, fundamentalists hold to their particular interpretation of these works as the supreme truth and condemn all deviations from it as a sin. Written words are seen as the ultimate spiritual authority. In many instances a form of idolatry takes place, in which sacred books are themselves worshiped as if they were God Himself.

The mystical view is quite different. Although holding scripture in no less esteem, mystics see holy texts as a sacred guide to a spiritual knowledge beyond the scope of words – a doorway to the same sort of personal revelation with which the authors of the scriptures were blessed. While fundamentalists quote scripture to shore up their dogmas and oppose them to others, mystics draw on scriptures as the inspiration for a spiritual adventure beyond the written word, to a direct experience of the truth.

From the fundamentalist perspective, religions are in a state of unavoidable competition, with only their particular viewpoint endorsed by God. From the mystics' perspective, the same truth can be stated in different conceptual languages. What matters is that a religion leads an individual to the true destination, which may itself be described in different ways. Ultimately the truth cannot be captured with words.

Fundamentalism, usually fueled by scriptural writings, has led to many of the horrendous religious conflicts that have bedeviled human history. The mystical understanding, often drawing on the same scriptural inspiration, can help overcome these tragic divisions.

This book stands boldly in the mystical tradition. It does not claim that all religions are the same; obviously they are not. Their various doctrines lead to endless theological debates within each religion, let alone between different religions. However, there are many essential points of profound agreement between faiths.

The whole notion of difference or similarity is, after all, a matter of perspective. Viewed close up, every human face is unique; yet viewed more abstractly, each contains a mouth, two eyes, and a nose. Are faces the same or different? They are both. In the same way, from a mystical perspective, the core spiritual understandings at the heart of every religious tradition can be seen to be essentially the same, although the conceptual and cultural forms they take are unique and individual.

The world has become a smaller place, and religions now have the chance to inform and debate with each other, to explore the universal spiritual understanding that human beings have discovered and rediscovered from time immemorial. This universal wisdom can not and should not replace the diversity of beliefs and practices which comprise distinct religious traditions. This would produce a dull and impoverished religious

ABOVE
The Playfair Book of Hours, *French, late 15th century.*

ABOVE
Thanka showing the Bodhisattva Ghantapani surrounded by incarnations of Buddha.

Comprehend one philosophical view through study of another one.

JAINISM:
ACARANGASUTRA
5.113

monoculture. However, an appreciation of the commonality between faiths allows a meeting place where traditions that have historically seen themselves as in opposition can develop mutual respect based on a shared spiritual understanding.

SCRIPTURES OF THE WORLD

Never before have so many sacred scriptures been readily available in English translation. The variety of texts that could be included in this book is enormous. The scriptures of Theravada Buddhists alone are eleven times as long as the Bible! I have not been able to present even short extracts from all of the influential scriptures of the world, let alone spiritual gems which are less familiar and often overlooked. I have, however, included a number of extracts from the scriptures of the major religions, as well as some quotations from smaller religions, ancient spiritual traditions, and the oral wisdom of preliterate cultures.

The religions of the East generally do not have a limited and organized canon of scripture and revere a monumental body of works, including later commentaries on older scriptures and the works of saints and sages influential in the development of their different traditions. I have drawn on many of these. Orthodox Judaism, Christianity, and Islam have strict canonical bodies of writings that are regarded as scripture, but to give a wider picture I have also included works from unorthodox sects within these traditions. When presenting dates I have avoided the Christian terms B.C. and A.D., in favor of the modern terms C.E. (Common Era) and B.C.E. (Before the Common Era), which are interchangeable with the old convention but a little less partisan.

Jewish scripture comprises the Tanakh and the Talmud. The Tanakh is the Old Testament of the Christians, but this name is foreign to Judaism, suggesting as it does a New Testament to follow it. The Tanakh comprises 39 books, divided into Torah (the Law), Nebi'im (the Prophets) and Ketuvim (the Writings). It was composed over a period of more than thirteen centuries from the time of the prophet Moses. The Talmud contains a tradition of oral Torah said to have developed with the return of the Jewish people from captivity in Babylon in about 583 B.C.E. It is not a single book, but two fabulous libraries of works, the Palestinian Talmud, edited in Jerusalem in about 400 B.C.E., and the Babylonian Talmud, edited in the Academies of Babylonia in about 500 B.C.E. I have also included extracts from scriptures known as the Dead Sea Scrolls, which were discovered in 1947 and belonged to a Jewish group called the Essenes who were contemporaries of Jesus, as well as poems from the beautiful Odes of Solomon, a Syriac text discovered in a Jewish hymnbook in 1909.

The canonical Christian scripture is the Bible, made up of the Old and New Testaments. Apart from the inclusion of a few extra books in some Bibles, the Old Testament is largely identical to the Jewish scripture, with

ABOVE
A landscape in the Haboku style by Sesshu (1420-1506).

its books reordered to emphasize the prophetic tradition which is believed to announce the coming of Jesus Christ. The New Testament contains four Gospels relating the story and teachings of Jesus, as well as letters and acts of the Apostles and the Book of Revelation. These books were selected as canonical scriptures from a wealth of gospels and sacred Christian writings in the fourth century by the Roman Church.

Other Christian schools and their scriptures were largely persecuted out of existence. The discovery in 1945 of scriptures belonging to heretical Gnostic Christians, however, has given us new insights into early Christianity, and I have included extracts from these extraordinary works. There are also quotations from The Gospel of Peace of Jesus Christ, a first-century Aramaic manuscript taken east to Asia by Nestorian Christian priests, as well as the works of Pseudo-Dionysius, traditionally said to have been written by Dionysius, a contemporary of St. Paul, but whose real author is unknown. Although not technically scriptures these latter writings have been so influential on the mystical tradition within Christianity that they deserve inclusion.

The Qur'an is the fundamental scripture of Islam. Unlike the scriptures of other religions, it is a single book with a single author. Its 114 suras are said to have been recited in Arabic to Muhammad (*c.*570–632 C.E.) by the angel Gabriel, and no translation into any other language is believed to capture its power and many levels of meaning. Islam is split into two sects, Sunni and Shiite. Sunni Muslims regard the traditional sayings of the Prophet as recollected and recorded by his companions as scriptures. These are called Hadith. The Shiite tradition also has a collection of Hadith, almost identical to the Sunni collection, but Shiites do not regard these as having scriptural authority. Shiite Muslims particularly revere Ali (d.661 C.E.), the son-in-law of Muhammad who became the fourth Caliph. They regard the Nahjul Balagha, a collection of Ali's teachings, as a sacred work. Although not technically scriptures, I have also included extracts from Rumi and other Sufi Muslims to represent this mystical school of Islamic spirituality.

Hinduism has a long and rich history of sacred writings. The most ancient texts are the Shruti or revealed scriptures: the four books of the Vedas, which were transmitted orally from the third millennium B.C.E., and later books called the Brahmanas and Upanishads. The Smriti scriptures, meaning "that which is remembered," include collections of duties and laws, such as the Laws of Manu, collections of philosophy and spiritual stories such as the Srimad Bhagavatam, as well as the two great Hindu epic narratives, the Ramayana and the Mahabharata. The latter of these contains the beautiful and influential Bhagavad Gita or Song of God. Hindu scripture also includes Vedanta, commentaries on the wisdom of the Vedas by later sages. I have included extracts from the Ashtavakra Gita and the works of the sage Sankara (788–820 B.C.E.).

Buddhism stems from the teachings of an Indian sage who became known as the Buddha (*c.*581–501 B.C.E.). There are two major Buddhist traditions. Theravada or The Teaching of the Elders is prevalent in Sri Lanka and

Those who praise their own doctrines and disparage the doctrines of others do not solve any problem.

JAINISM:
SUTRAKRITANGA
1.1.50

Southeast Asia. Mahayana or The Greater Vehicle developed in Tibet, Mongolia, China, Korea, and Japan. The canon of Theravada scriptures is written in Pali and is called the Tripitaka or Three Baskets. The Vinaya Pitaka is concerned with the Sangha or Buddhist community. The Sutta Pitaka consists of discourses of the Buddha. The Abhimdhamma Pitaka consists of analyses of Buddhist teachings. The most well-known and popular Theravada scripture is the Dhammapada or Verses of Righteousness. Mahayana scriptures are even more numerous than Theravada scriptures. Many of the different schools of Mahayana Buddhism have their own works which they regard as central. This vast body of scripture was originally written in Sanskrit and collected into Tibetan and Chinese Tripitakas. It includes major new sutras such as the famous Lotus Sutra, the wisdom literature known as the Prajnaparamita, and devotional literature such as the Pure Land Sutra. I have also included extracts from works belonging to the meditation school, known in Japan as Zen.

The foremost Taoist text is the Tao Te Ching by a legendary sage called Lao Tzu (6th–5th centuries B.C.E.). Other great Taoist works are by the mysterious master Chuang Tzu (4th–3rd centuries B.C.E.), and the slightly later master Lieh Tzu. I have also included extracts from two other Taoist books, the Tai-Shang Kan-Ying P'ien (Treatise on Repose and Retribution) and the Yin Chih Wen (Tract of the Quiet Way).

Confucianism was inspired by the Chinese sage Confucius (551–479 B.C.E.). Its canonical scriptures are the Five Classics and the Four Books. The Five Classics are ancient books which Confucius himself studied, including the Book of Songs, the Book of History, the Spring and Autumn Annals, the Book of Rituals, and the Book of Changes, known in the West by its Chinese name, the I Ching. The Four Books are the Analects by Confucius himself, the Great Learning, the Doctrine of the Mean, and a book by Confucius' greatest successor Mencius (372–289 B.C.E.), named after its author.

I have also included extracts from smaller religious traditions. Zoroastrianism, founded by the prophet Zarathustra (c.1000 B.C.E.), was once a major and influential Persian religion which is now practiced by less than 100,000 Parsees, mostly in India. Its scripture is the Avesta, the main text of which is called the Yasna, at the heart of which are the Gathas, hymns composed by Zarathustra and his close disciples.

Jainism was founded by Mahavira (599–527 B.C.E.), who is regarded as 24th in a long succession of enlightened Tirthankaras or Fordfinders, extending back to the sage Rishabhadeva who is mentioned in the ancient Hindu Vedas. There are two Jain traditions, each holding different scriptures as having spiritual authority.

The sacred book of the Sikhs is the Adi Granath. It comprises the writings of Guru Nanak (1469–1539 C.E.) who was the inspiration of Sikhism, and the five Gurus who succeeded him. It was compiled by Guru Arjan Dev, the fifth in the line of succession. Guru Gobind Singh, the tenth and last great Sikh master, deemed this scripture to be the Guru Granth Shib

Like the bees gathering honey from different flowers, the wise accept the essence of different scriptures and see only the good in all religions.

HINDUISM:
SRIMAD
BHAGAVATAM

ABOVE
Portrait of Hermes Trismegistus, after Jacques Bossard.

– The Eternal Living Guru. Since this time the Adi Granath scripture has itself been venerated by Sikhs as the Guru.

I have also presented extracts from the scriptures of new religions such as the Baha'i faith, which grew out of Islam, and from modern Japanese faiths such as Omoto Kyo, Tenrikyo, Seicho-no-le, and Perfect Liberty Kyodan, which are syncretic hybrids of Shinto and other religions. Shinto, the indigenous religion of Japan, has no written scriptures as such, but I have included extracts from some of its writings.

There are in excess of 100 million followers of indigenous religions which have no written scriptures, so I felt it right that their oral wisdom also be represented. Although officially dead traditions, the ancient pagan mystery religions have played such an influential role on Western spirituality that I have also included extracts from the writings of their great sages such as Hermes Trismegistus, Heraclitus, and Plotinus.

THE PROBLEM OF TRANSLATION

Scripture must speak directly to our soul, if it is to have the transforming impact its authors intended. Old-fashioned language can give sacred texts an air of authority, but it also makes them seem pompous and distant. I have taken the liberty of reworking translations that are archaic sounding to increase their immediacy and return to them the sense that, although speaking from the distant past, they address our current situation.

The fact that these texts come to us in translation at all is a major obstacle to understanding. We are limited by the level of insight of the translator as well as our own. The language of scripture often contains depths of meaning that are easily lost. The extent of this problem is brought out by Neil Douglas-Klotz, whose insights I have drawn on a number of times in this book. In *Prayers of the Cosmos* and *Desert Wisdom* (HarperSanFrancisco, 1994 and 1995), Douglas-Klotz points out, for example, that the words in Hebrew, Aramaic, and Arabic scriptures which are commonly translated as "heaven" do not denote a metaphysical place – heaven as opposed to earth. Rather, they embrace a wide range of mystical meanings, such as "vibration" or "light and sound shining through creation." Read with this understanding, familiar biblical lines take on a completely new meaning.

As translations of the scriptures improve, their deeper spiritual meaning emerges and their common ground becomes plainer. It could well turn out that all that ever divided the spirituality of different religions was the misunderstanding caused by language. For now, we must be thankful for the extraordinary work that has been done by scholars and linguists to make so much of the world's spiritual resources available to us, even though sometimes in less than perfect form. These imperfections can be compensated for by approaching these texts with an open mind. Don't assume that sacred writings mean what others say they mean. Look deeper. Resonate with them and penetrate their meaning for yourself. Take them

ABOVE
Title page of the Great Bible, c. 1539.

To be attached to a certain view and to look down upon other views as inferior – this the wise man calls a fetter.

BUDDHISM:
SUTTA NIPATA
798

into your heart and meditate on them, and they will reward you with insight and revelation.

Adopting a mystical approach to scripture liberates us from the tyranny of the written word and opens us to discovering the underlying spirit. It not only builds bridges between different traditions, allowing them to complement rather than confront each other, but also sets us free to play a little, without feeling we are being sacrilegious or compromising the truth. Scriptures from distant cultures contain ideas that may be unfamiliar to Western readers. Those which are common in our culture, such as extracts from the Bible, may be colored by over-familiarity, and their true meaning obscured. To bring freshness to the familiar and allow insight into the exotic, it is revealing to experiment with moving terms from one tradition into a scripture of a different tradition.

The familiar words of Jesus from the New Testament "I am the Way and the Life," could be rendered "I am the Tao and the Te," as they often are in Chinese translation. This immediately makes Jesus sound like a Zen Master, rather than the traditional Jewish "man of sorrows," and calls into question our present cultural assumptions about the nature of the man and his teachings. Likewise, the famous beginning to Lao Tzu's Tao Te Ching is usually rendered into English as "The Tao that can be spoken of is not the true Tao." The concepts Tao and God are both broad terms and are not necessarily synonymous. However, if the word *God* is taken in its most abstract and ineffable sense, this sentence could be rendered, "The God that can be spoken of is not the true God." This immediately makes Lao Tzu's thought more accessible to those to whom the word *Tao* is strange or confusing.

Although every religion has a unique philosophy which uses a particular vocabulary, exchanging terms from different traditions can open new ways into the universal wisdom at their heart. Simple terms to interchange are the words used to denote the Supreme Oneness, such as *Tao* (Taoism), *Allah* (Islam), *Brahman* (Hinduism), and *Dharma*, *Buddha-Nature*, or *Suchness* (Buddhism). Experimenting with such substitutions while you contemplate the scriptures in this book can reveal unexpected levels of meaning. In my commentaries I have generally used the familiar word *God*, but it can often be replaced with terms from other traditions.

A COMMON HUMAN SPIRITUALITY

The scriptures are a deep well of wisdom that can never be plumbed, yet within which our questions reverberate, awakening the soul to awe and wonder. Often confusing and confronting, holy writings challenge our assumptions about the fundamental truths of life. They urge us to look again and always to remember the profound mystery of existence.

Each tradition offers something unique and yet essentially similar. Is this really surprising? Aren't people of every race and time different and yet

ABOVE
Tibetan thanka showing a Buddhist mandala.

universally human? If our common ground is to be found anywhere, it is in our spirituality which takes us beyond the apparent separateness of things to a vision of oneness, lifting us beyond our personal differences to the unifying knowledge of God. This is the supreme task of sacred scripture. As it says in the Srimad Bhagavatam:

Truth has many aspects. Infinite truth has infinite expressions. Though the sages speak in diverse ways, they express one and the same Truth. The ignorant say, "What I believe is true; others are wrong." It is because of this attitude of the ignorant that there have been doubts and misunderstandings about God. It is this attitude that causes dispute among men. But all doubts vanish when one masters the self and finds peace by realizing the heart of Truth. Thereupon dispute, too, is at an end.

HINDUISM: SRIMAD BHAGAVATAM 11.15

LEFT
An ornamental page from a Koran written and illuminated for the Sultan Uljaitu, 1310.

FAR LEFT
Jewish literary text from a collection of prayers.

CHAPTER ONE

The Supreme Being

THE ULTIMATE QUESTION addressed by scripture is the nature of the Supreme Being. Who or what is God? The major religions are often seen as divided into three strands, each with fundamentally opposing answers to this question. Judaism, Christianity, and Islam are regarded as monotheistic religions, which claim there is one God. Hinduism, popular Buddhism, indigenous traditions, and ancient pagan religions are regarded as polytheistic, believing in many gods and goddesses. Philosophical Buddhism and Taoism are regarded as nontheistic, believing there is no God. These differences, while interesting and important, blur and confuse an underlying unanimity. All traditions recognize a fundamental oneness, whether it is called *Yahweh* (Judaism), *God* (Christianity), *Allah* (Islam), *Brahman* (Hinduism), *Wakan Tanka* (Native American tradition), *Suchness* (Buddhism), or *Tao* (Taoism).

Each approach has insights to offer. The virtue of polytheism is that it acknowledges the Supreme Being as an impersonal, ineffable God, who can be approached through its many masks – the gods and goddesses who manifest different divine qualities. In Hinduism, for example, a devotee may follow the one God through an *ishta-deva* – a particular deity that suits one's personal needs and temperament. Monotheism avoids the clutter of many deities, but still traditionally replaces a diverse pantheon with angels and saints who fulfill a similar function. Orthodox Christianity also contains important polytheistic elements in its notion of the Holy Trinity or God in Three Persons – Father, Son, and Holy Spirit. Philosophical Buddhism and Taoism conceptualize the Supreme Being in a purely abstract way as the Suchness or Tao – the underlying reality or wholeness of things. These concepts, however, can seem distant and unapproachable, and popular forms of these faiths worship gods, buddhas, nature spirits, and the ancestors.

Whatever the tradition, two things are held in common. First, God is one. Second, human beings generally find this oneness more easy to relate to if it is pictured with a human face.

OPPOSITE
French stained glass showing the creation of the sun, moon, and stars.

THE ONENESS OF GOD

All religious traditions turn to the language of unity to express the nature of the Supreme Being. Translations often convey very little of the great depth of meaning expressed in the original language by the holy names given to the Supreme Being. *Adonai*, a biblical name for God, is usually translated "Lord." In Hebrew it suggests "the essential unity that divides to give life." Many Jewish and Islamic names for God are based around the root *el* or *al*, which conveys "The One" or "The All." *Elohim*, the name of God in the Hebrew book of Genesis, could be translated "The One That Is Many" or "The Being of Beings" or "The Consciousness in All." *Alaha*, the name of God in the Aramaic that Jesus spoke, could be rendered as "the One moving through all souls." *Allah*, the name of God used by Muhammad, combines the roots *al* and *la* to express "the Oneness of Being and Nothingness." The Hebrew name for God often transliterated *Yahweh* or *Jehovah* conveys "an eternal power that manifests in life" and "a door between existence and nonexistence."

The wise is One alone, unwilling and willing to be spoken of by the name Zeus.

ANCIENT MYSTERY RELIGIONS:
HERACLITUS CXVIII

There can be no doubt that whatever the peoples of the world, of whatever race or religion, they derive their inspiration from one heavenly Source, and are the subjects of one God. The difference between the ordinances under which they abide should be attributed to the varying requirements and exigencies of the age in which they were revealed. All of them, except for a few which are the outcome of human perversity, were ordained of God, and are a reflection of His Will and Purpose.

BAHA'I FAITH: GLEANINGS FROM THE
WRITINGS OF BAHA'U'LLAH 1.11

*Truth is One and the learned call it
by many names*

HINDUISM: RIG VEDA

*Hear O Israel: the Lord our God
the Lord is One.*

JUDAISM AND CHRISTIANITY:
DEUTERONOMY 6.4

*Say,
He is God,
the One!
God,
the eternally besought of all!*

ISLAM: QUR'AN 112

*There is only one God; all the "gods"
are but His ministering angels who
are His manifestations.*

SHINTO: OMOTO KYO. MICHI-NO-SHIORI

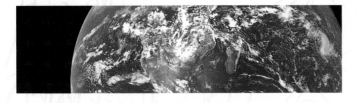

ABOVE
*View of Earth from
the* Apollo 17
spacecraft.

*Mysteriously existing
before Heaven and earth.
Silent and empty.
An unchanging oneness.
An everchanging presence.
The Mother of all Life.*

*It is impossible
to really give it a name,
but I call it Tao.
Without wishing to define it,
it could be called "The Whole."*

TAOISM: TAO TE CHING 25

*Every object in the world has a spirit
and that spirit is wakan. Thus the
spirits of the tree or things of that
kind, while not like the spirit of man,
are also wakan. Wakan comes from
the wakan beings. These wakan
beings are greater than mankind in
the same way that mankind is greater
than animals. They are never born
and never die. They can do many
things that mankind cannot do.
Mankind can pray to the wakan
beings for help. The word* Wakan
Tanka *means all of the wakan beings
because they are all as if one.*

INDIGENOUS RELIGIONS: SWORD, A NATIVE
AMERICAN DAKOTA

*One perfect Nature pervades and
circulates within all natures.
One all-inclusive Reality contains
and embraces all realities.
One moon is reflected in every
expanse of water.
Every reflected moon
is the one moon.
The essence of all the Buddhas
is in my being.
My essence is in their being.
The Inner Light is beyond
good and bad.
Like space it knows no boundaries.
It is here right now, within us,
always full and serene.
Only when you hunt for it
do you miss it.
You can't grasp it, but
you can't lose it.
It winds its own way.
When you are silent, it speaks.
When you speak, it is dumb.
There are no obstacles.
The great gate of love is wide open.*

BUDDHISM: ZEN MASTER
YUNG-CHIA TA-SHIH

ABOVE
*A Native American
image of the
Thunderbird, the
Supreme Being.*

THE INEFFABLE ONE

God is often compared to light and is experienced as such by mystics from the Christian St. Paul to the Indian saint Kabir. Like light, God illuminates all things. God is ineffable and beyond description. As it says in the Qur'an, "No vision can grasp Him, but His grasp is over all vision; He is above all comprehension, yet is acquainted with all things" (Qur'an 6.103). God knows all, yet is unknowable. In the Hermetica, an Egyptian scripture attributed to the ancient sage Hermes Trismegistus, Atum (God) is described as "hidden, yet obvious everywhere." "Mystified?" asks Lao Tzu. "Tao is mystery. This is the gateway to understanding."

ABOVE
The Earth Spider
Making Magic in the
Palace of Rai Rwo,
by Kuniyoshi.

Allah
is
the
one
light
that
illuminates
heaven
and earth.

ISLAM: THE QUR'AN 24

Him the sun does not illumine, nor the moon, nor the stars, nor the lightning, nor fires kindled upon the earth. He is the one light that gives light to all. He shines – everything shines.

HINDUISM: KATHA UPANISHAD 5.15

Tao is not a way
that can be pointed out.
Nor an idea that can be defined.

Tao is indefinable original totality.
Ideas create the appearance of
separate things.

Always hidden,
it is the mysterious essence.
Always manifest,
it is the outer appearances.

Essence and appearance are the same.
Only ideas
make them seem separate.
Mystified?

Tao is mystery.
This is the gateway to understanding.

TAOISM: TAO TE CHING 1

Can you find out
the deep things of God?
Can you find out
the limit of the Almighty?
It is higher than heaven –
what can you do?
Deeper than Sheol –
what can you know?
Its measure is longer than the earth,
and broader than the sea.

JUDAISM AND CHRISTIANITY: JOB 11.7–9

ABOVE
Chinese pictogram
meaning "all
things."

Praise be to God, who knows the secrets of all things and proofs of whose existence shine in various phases of nature. No physical eye has nor will ever see Him. But those who have not seen Him physically cannot deny His existence, yet the minds of those who have accepted His existence cannot grasp the real essence of the Divine Nature.

His place is so high that nothing can be imagined higher. He is so near to us that nothing can be nearer. The eminence of His position has not placed Him any further away from His creatures, and His nearness has not brought them on a par with Him.

He has not permitted the human mind to grasp the essence of His Being, yet He has not prevented them from realizing His presence. Various aspects of the universe force even atheists to accept Him as its Grand Architect, yet He is far above the conceptions of those who refuse His existence, and also of those who imagine His attributes in various expressions of nature.

ISLAM: NAHJUL BALAGHA, SERMON 54

ABOVE
Detail of a papyrus of Nespakashuty, showing the god Geb separated from his wife, the goddess Nut, 1040-959 B.C.E.

Who can fathom the designs of Your heart? Apart from You nothing has existed, and without Your will nothing will be; yet none can understand Your wisdom nor gaze upon Your secrets.

JUDAISM: DEAD SEA SCROLLS

BELOW
Vishnu Visvarupa represented as the whole world, Jaipur, early 19th century.

To conceive of Atum is difficult. To define him is impossible. The imperfect and impermanent cannot easily apprehend the eternally perfected. Atum is whole and constant. In himself he is motionless, yet he is self-moving. He is immaculate, incorruptible and ever-lasting. He is the Supreme Absolute Reality. He is filled with ideas which are imperceptible to the senses, and with all-embracing Knowledge. Atum is Primal Mind.

He is too great to be called by the name "Atum." He is hidden, yet obvious everywhere. His Being is known through thought alone, yet we see his form before our eyes. He is bodiless, yet embodied in everything. There is nothing which he is not. He has no name, because all names are his name. He is the unity in all things, so we must know him by all names and call everything "Atum."

ANCIENT MYSTERY RELIGIONS: HERMETICA

MOTHER AND FATHER

Many faiths hold that the Supreme Being is the creator of the universe, often imagined as a cosmic parent. He/She is the source of life, who continually loves and nurtures his/her creation. The monotheistic religions have flourished in patriarchal societies and have come to emphasize the image of God as divine father. But many names for God interpreted as male are not actually gender-specific. Jesus called God *Abwoon*, an Aramaic term normally translated "father," for example. But it could equally well be rendered in a gender-neutral way as "parent" or "mother-father" or even "the breath of life that comes from the All."

It is not uncommon, however, for the Creator to be seen as male and associated with the spiritual heavens, while the female aspect of divinity is embodied in materiality and often seen as Mother Earth. As human beings we are both spirit and matter and share in the nature of both. The primal void which in some traditions is seen to preexist God is often also portrayed as feminine. In the Tao Te Ching, for example, Lao Tzu talks of the Tao as the Mother of all things. In mainstream Christianity, the image of the Mother has played only a minor role, but as can be seen in The Thunder, Perfect Mind and the extraordinary Aramaic text The Gospel of Peace of Jesus Christ, the Divine Feminine is not overlooked in all Christian traditions.

ABOVE
Vishnu represented as the whole world.

*I am Father and Mother
of the world.
The Great Principle, the Divine,
is my womb;
I cast the seed into it;
There is the origin of all creatures.
Whatever forms originate
in any wombs
the real womb is the Divine,
the Great Principle.
I am the Father that gives the seed.*

HINDUISM: BHAGAVAD GITA 9.17 AND
14.3–4

LEFT
A Japanese goddess.

*All you under heaven! Regard
heaven as your father, earth as your
mother, and all things as your
brothers and sisters.*

SHINTO: ORACLE OF ATSUTA

You are Father, Mother,
Friend, Brother,
With You
as succourer in all places,
what fear have I?

SIKHISM:

ADI GRANTH MAJH M.5

LEFT
The Immaculate
Conception,
*Francisco de
Zurbaran
(1598-1664).*

*Your Mother is in you, and you in
her. She bore you; she gives you life.
It was she who gave to you your
body, and to her shall you one day
give it back again.*

*The blood which runs in us is born of
the blood of our Earthly Mother. Her
blood falls from the clouds; leaps up
from the womb of the earth; babbles
in the brooks of the mountains; flows
wide in the rivers of the plains; sleeps
in the lakes; rages mightily in the
tempestuous seas.*

*The air which we breathe is born of
the breath of our Earthly Mother.
Her breath is azure in the heights of
the heavens; soars in the tops of the
mountains; whispers in the leaves of
the forest; billows over the cornfields;
slumbers in the deep valleys; burns
hot in the desert.*

*The tenderness of our flesh is born of
the flesh of our Earthly Mother;
whose flesh waxes yellow and red in
the fruits of the trees, and nurtures us
in the furrows of the fields.*

*The light of our eyes, the hearing of
our ears, both are born of the colors
and the sounds of our Earthly
Mother; which enclose us about, as
the waves of the sea a fish, as the
eddying air a bird.*

*I tell you truly, you are one with the
Earthly Mother.*

CHRISTIANITY: THE GOSPEL OF PEACE OF

JESUS CHRIST

RIGHT
The Tree of Jesse,
*Romanian, 16th
century.*

THE WORD OF GOD

The concept of the Word is found in many scriptures. It is sometimes taken to refer to scripture itself, but it has a deeper metaphysical meaning. Whether it is the Hindu *Om* or the ancient Greek *Logos*, the Word is a symbol of the primal vibration through which the universe manifests. It is God's first thought which fashions all that is. It is, as it says in the Hermetica, "The idea of beautiful order."

Hermes Trismegistus relates his mystical vision of the Word calming and organizing the primal chaos. He calls the Word "the Son of God." In the Christian tradition Jesus Christ is regarded as the Son of God who is "the Word made flesh." The Word is the essential nature of all that is. In the Hermetica and the Greek New Testament the untranslated term used is *Logos* which is often translated as "reason." It is the power which differentiates the Oneness into multiplicity.

The concept of the Word may seem strange and opaque, but if we think about our own experience, it begins to make sense. Words spring mysteriously into our minds, just as creation springs miraculously from nothingness. With words we shape and understand our reality, dividing the oneness of life into individual entities which we can name. As it says in the Tao Te Ching, "Ideas create the world of separate things." Likewise, the Buddhist Dhammapada teaches "with our thoughts we make the world." Just as ideas appear in our personal minds to shape the reality we perceive, so God's Word appears in his Universal Mind to manifest creation.

BELOW
*Christ enthroned
with the gospels.*

*I*n the beginning was the Word, and the Word was with God, and the Word was God. He was in the beginning with God; all things were made through him, and without him was not anything made that was made.

CHRISTIANITY: JOHN

1.1–4

*I*n the beginning was the only Lord of the Universe. His Word (Om) was with him. This Word was his second. He contemplated. He said, "I will deliver this Word so that she will produce and bring into being all this world."

HINDUISM: TANDYA MAHA BRAHMANA

20.14.2

ABOVE
*Vishnu plans the
cosmic order by
causing demons and
gods to haul on the
Sesha cosmic serpent.*

I will tell you the Word that all the Vedas glorify, all self-sacrifice expresses, all sacred studies and holy life seek. That Word is Om.

HINDUISM: KATHA UPANISHAD

*In the beginning was God,
Today is God
Tomorrow will be God.
Who can make an image of God?
He has no body.
He is as a word
which comes out of your mouth.
That word!
It is no more.
It is past, and still it lives!
So is God.*

INDIGENOUS RELIGIONS: PYGMY HYMN FROM
ZAIRE

*Suddenly
everything changed before me.
Reality was opened out in a moment.
I saw the boundless view.
All became dissolved in Light –
united within one joyous Love.
Yet the Light cast a shadow,
grim and terrible,
which, passing downwards,
became like restless water,
chaotically tossing forth spume
like smoke.
And I heard an unspeakable lament –
an inarticulate cry of separation.
The Light then uttered a Word,
which calmed the chaotic waters.*

*My Guide asked:
"Do you understand
the secrets of this vision?
I am that Light – the Mind of God,
which exists before
the chaotic dark waters
of potentiality.
My calming Word is the Son of God –
the idea of beautiful order;
the harmony of all things
with all things.
Primal Mind is parent of the Word,
just as in your own experience,
your human mind
gives birth to speech.
They cannot be divided,
one from the other,
for life is the union
of Mind and Word."*

ANCIENT MYSTERY RELIGIONS: HERMETICA

ABOVE
*Scenes from the life
of Krishna.*

LEFT
*From a decorative
script book of* Stories
from the Life of
Muhammad.

THE ALL-EMBRACING ONE

The Supreme Being is all embracing. The Muslims employ ninety-nine sublime names of Allah to capture some of his transcendent attributes. In the Hindu Bhagavad Gita, the warrior Arjuna discovers that his charioteer Krishna is actually an embodiment of the Supreme Being who blesses Arjuna with a cosmic vision of the awesome scope of his Divine Nature. In The Thunder, Perfect Mind, a remarkable scripture of the Gnostic Christians, a Divine Feminine voice describes herself as embracing all opposites and contradictions, including that which is loathed and despised. The Taoist sage Chuang Tzu explains that the Tao permeates everything, right down to excrement and urine.

*O Lord, I see within your body all
the gods and every kind of
living creature.
I see Brahma, the Creator, seated
upon a lotus; I see the ancient sages
and celestial serpents.*

*I see infinite mouths, arms, stomachs,
and eyes, and you are embodied in
every form. I see you everywhere,
without beginning, middle, or end.
You are the Lord of all creation, and
the cosmos is your body.*

*You wear a crown and carry a mace
and discus; your radiance is blinding
and immeasurable. I see you, who
are so difficult to behold, shining like
a fiery sun blazing in every direction.*

*You are the supreme, changeless
reality, the one thing to be known.
You are the refuge of all creation, the
immortal spirit, the eternal guardian
of eternal dharma.*

*Your presence fills the heavens
and earth, which tremble before this
vision of your wonderful
and terrible form*

HINDUISM: BHAGAVAD GITA CHAP. 11

*Tung-kuo Tzu asked Chuang Tzu,
"What is Tao? Where is it?"
"It is everywhere,"
replied Chuang Tzu.
Tung-kuo Tzu said,
"Can you be more specific."
"It's in an ant," said Chuang Tzu.
"Is it so low?"
"It's in a weed."
"Why that's even lower."
"It's in broken pottery."
"Still lower!"
"It's in excrement and urine," said
Chuang Tzu.
Tung-kuo gave no response.
"Sir," said Chuang Tzu, "your
question doesn't go to the heart of the
matter. When inspector Huo asked
the superintendent of markets about
the fatness of pigs, the tests were
always made in parts less and less
likely to be fat. Do not insist on Tao
being any particular thing. Nothing
escapes from Tao. Such is perfect Tao
– Complete, Entire, and All. These
are three different words, but they
mean the same thing. They all
designate the One."*

TAOISM: CHUANG TZU 22

ABOVE
*Chi Rho page –
"Beginning," from
The Book of Kells.*

Allah, the Name that is above every name.
al-Awwal, the First, who was before the beginning.
al-Akhir, the Last, who will still be after all has ended.
al-Badi', the Contriver, who contrived the whole art of creation.
al-Bari', the Maker, from whose hand we all come.
al-Barr, the Beneficent, whose liberality appears in all His works.
al-Basir, the Observant, who sees and hears all things.
al-Basit, the Spreader, who extends His mercy to whom He wills.
al-Batin, the Inner, who is immanent within all things.
al-Ba'ith, the Raiser, who will raise up a witness from each community.
al-Hafiz, the Guardian, who keeps watch over everything.
al-Haqq, the Truth.
al-Hakim, the Wise, who is both wise and well informed.
al-Halim, the Kindly, who is both forgiving and kindly disposed.
al-Hamid, the Praiseworthy, to whom all praise is due.
al-Hayy, the Living, who is the source of all life.
al-Khafid, the Humbler, who humbles some while He exalts others.
al-Khaliq, the Creator, who has created all things that are.
al-Ra'uf, the Gentle, who is compassionate toward His people.
al-Rahman, the Merciful, the most merciful of those who show mercy.
al-Rahim, the Compassionate, who is gentle and full of compassion.
al-Razzaq, the Provider, who provides but asks no provision.
al-Rashid, the Guide, who leads believers in the right-minded way.
al-Salam, the Peace-Maker, whose name is Peace.
al-Shakur, the Grateful, who graciously accepts the service of His people.
al-Shahid, the Witness, who is witness to all things.
al-Sabur, the Forbearing, who has great patience with His people.
al-Samad, the Eternal, who begets not and is not begotten.
al-Fattah, the Opener, who clears and opens up the Way.
al-Kabir, the Great One, who is both high and great.

ISLAM: A SELECTION FROM MUHAMMAD AL-MADANI'S NINETY-NINE

MOST BEAUTIFUL NAMES OF ALLAH

LEFT
Muhammad allows four tribes to lift the black stone into position at Al-Ka'ba.

Don't be unaware of me,
anywhere or at anytime.

For I am the beginning and the end.
I am both whore and holy.
I am wife and virgin.
I am barren and fertile.
I am bride and bridegroom.
My husband is my father,
and I am his mother.

I am the incomprehensible silence
and the idea that cannot be forgotten.

I am knowledge and ignorance.
I am ashamed and shameless.
I am bold and frightened.
I am war and peace.
Listen to me –
I am the disgraced and the respected.

Recognize my poverty and riches.
Don't arrogantly dismiss me
when I am despised,
and you will find me.
Don't point at me
when I'm on the dung heap,
and leave me reviled,
and you will find me.
Don't laugh at me
when I am disgraced and humbled.
Don't detest me,
when I am violently killed.
For I am compassion and I am
cruelty.

Be aware.
Don't hate my disobedience
and don't love my self-discipline.
Don't forsake me in my weakness
and don't fear my power.
Why do you not value my terror
and curse my pride?

I am She – present in all fear.
I am strength in trembling.
I am senseless and wise.

I am the one you have despised,
yet you venerate me.
I am the one you hide from,
yet I still see you.
But when you hide from yourself –
I will appear to you.
And when you appear –
I will hide from you.

I am control and uncontrollable
I am sentence and acquittal.
I am sinless and the root of all sin.
Everyone can hear me,
but no one can understand me.
Listen to my gentleness,
and learn from my roughness.
I am She who cries out.

Hear me then, you who are listening,
and you angels and messengers,
and spirits arisen from the dead.
I am the One who alone exists.

CHRISTIANITY: GNOSTIC GOSPEL, THE
THUNDER, PERFECT MIND

BEFORE GOD

Most children who have been told that God created the world ask the logical question, "So, where did God come from?" The Rig Veda questions whether even God knows the answer.

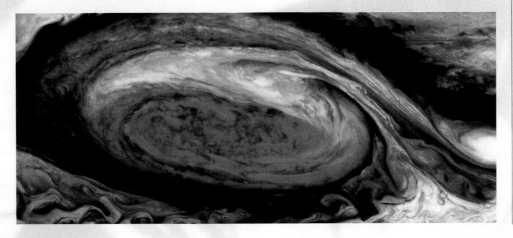

*Then there was neither existence
      nor nothingness.
      There was no sky
      or heaven beyond it.
What was there? What power? Who?
Was there unfathomable depths
      of water?
Then there was neither death
      nor immortality.
Neither the torch of day nor night.
The One breathed unmoving
      and self-sustaining.
There was the One and no other.
Darkness wrapped in darkness.
All was fluid and formless.
In the void of Oneness
      arose the fire of fervor;
Love, the primal seed.
Seeking wisdom in their hearts,
The sages have seen this truth –
The bond of union between being
      and non-being.*

*But, when all is said and done,
Who can say how it all happened?
The gods themselves
      are later than creation,
So who really knows
      how things came to be.
What is the origin of creation?
Only the highest God knows
      whence it all came –
Whether it was made or is uncreated.
      He knows –
or may be even He doesn't know.*

HINDUISM: RIG VEDA X.129

THE VOID

Many traditions teach that before there was a creator god, there was a void or plenum – nothingness containing the potential for everything. Christians call this the *Godhead*. Lao Tzu calls it the mysterious *Tao*. Hindus call it *Brahman* as distinct from *Brahma* who is God the Creator. In Hindu thought, Brahman is Pure Consciousness aware of nothing. He becomes aware as the Atman or One Self that is conscious through all beings. From this Primal Consciousness, Brahma the creator god himself arises.

The Buddha was loath to get tied up in metaphysical speculations, preferring to point his followers to the possibility of directly experiencing the void for themselves – an experience he called "Nirvana." *Nirvana* is an awareness of consciousness itself, within which everything exists as a thought. It is the no thing which contains all things.

LEFT
Shakyamuni's entrance into perfect Nirvana.

*For those in mid-stream,
in great peril of the flood;
For those adventuring
on ageing and dying –
I proclaim the isle where is no-thing,
where naught is grasped.
This is the Isle of no-beyond:
I call it Nirvana – the utter extinction
of ageing and dying.*

BUDDHISM: SUTTANIPATTA 1093–4

BUDDHISM: SAMYUTTA-NIKAYA II, 117

*Tao is like an empty space,
that can never be filled up.
Yet it contains everything:
Blunt and sharp,
resolved and confused,
bright and dull,
the whole of Creation.*

*Hidden, but always present.
Who created it?
It existed before the Creator.*

TAOISM: TAO TE CHING 4

When appearances and names are put away and all discrimination ceases, that which remains is the true and essential nature of things and, as nothing can be predicated as to the nature of essence, it is called the "Suchness" of Reality.

This universal, undifferentiated, inscrutable Suchness is the only Reality, but it is variously characterized as Nirvana, Truth, Mind-essence, Transcendental Intelligence, Perfection of Wisdom, and so on.

This Dharma of the imagelessness of the Essence-nature of Ultimate Reality is the Dharma which has been proclaimed by all the Buddhas, and when all things are understood in full agreement with it, one is in possession of Perfect Knowledge.

BUDDHISM: LANKAVATARA SUTRA 83

As the web issues out of the spider, as plants sprout from the earth, as hair grows from the body, so the sages say, this universe springs from the deathless Self – the source of life. The deathless Self meditated upon Himself and projected the universe as evolutionary energy. From this energy developed life, mind, the elements, and the world of karma, which is enchained by cause and effect. The deathless Self sees all and knows all. From Him springs Brahma, who embodies the process of evolution into name and form, by which the One appears to be many.

HINDUISM: MUNDAKA UPANISHAD 1.1.7–9

CHAPTER TWO

The Self

T HE FUNDAMENTAL HUMAN QUESTION is "Who or what am I?" Scriptures agree that we are not the mortal body that we may take ourselves to be; rather, our essential nature is immortal and eternal. The Jewish, Christian, and Muslim traditions say we are a soul made in the image of God. The Hindu tradition claims that Atman is Brahman – the Self is God. The Buddhist responds that the self is an illusion and does not exist at all. At first these may seem like contradictory answers, but underlying them all is a common spiritual perception expressed in different ways. This can be illustrated by a Zen Buddhist teaching story.

A Chinese Empress asked a master about the relationship between the One and the many. In response he put mirrors all around a room and lit a candle in the middle. The Empress was moved by the splendor of the reflected light. The sage explained that the candle was the One and the reflections were the many.

The responses of the major religions are like descriptions of this metaphor. The Jewish, Christian, and Muslim traditions say that God is the candle, and we humans are the images in the mirrors. The Hindu tradition points out that the candle and its reflection are actually the same light and therefore identical. The Buddhist tradition reminds us that a reflection is only a reflection and is in reality an illusion; there is only one light.

OPPOSITE
The Buddha,
*Odilon Redon
(1840-1916).*

IMAGES OF THE SOUL

Where is God to be found? Most scriptures answer, "within." God is not remote and inaccessible, but closer than we can possibly imagine. God lives in us. The body is like a temple which houses an eternal spirit. Humanity is the meeting place of the Immortal and the mortal, of Consciousness and matter. The soul is God within us.

In the Hebrew book of Genesis, God says, "Let us make man in our image." The Hebrew word translated "man" denotes an archetypal human being, not a male body, and the Hebrew translated "in our image" suggests an image or picture projected by light. The essence of human nature, the soul, is a light projected from the Light of God. It is consciousness arising from the Supreme Consciousness.

This is a wonderful,
unique discourse:
The living Self
is the image
of the Supreme Being.
It is neither old nor a child.
It neither suffers pain
nor is caught in death's snare.
It neither shatters nor dies.
It pervades all time.
It feels neither heat nor cold.
It has neither friend nor foe.
It feels neither joy nor sorrow:
It owns all and is all-powerful.
It has neither father
nor mother.
It has always existed
beyond the limits of matter.
It is touched by neither sin
nor goodness.
It is ever awake
within the heart
of every being.

SIKHISM: ADI GRANTH, GAUND M.5

And God said,
Let us make man in our image.

JUDAISM AND CHRISTIANITY: GENESIS 1:26

Beloved is man, for he was created in the image of God. But it was by a special love that it was made known to him that he was created in the image of God.

JUDAISM: ABOT 3.18

Just as God fills the whole world, so the soul fills the body. Just as God sees, but is not seen, so the soul sees, but is not itself seen. Just as God feeds the whole world, so the soul feeds the whole body. Just as God is pure, so the soul is pure. Just as God dwells in the innermost precincts of the Temple, so also the soul dwells in the innermost part of the body.

JUDAISM: BERAKOT 10A

If we keep unperverted the human heart which is like heaven and received from earth – that is God.

SHINTO: REVELATION TO EMPEROR SEIWA

LEFT
A mosaic of the head of Christ, Turkish, 12th century.

Rabbi Tanhuma said: "A man's soul informs the Recording Angel of his every deed. It is like a nobleman, who has married the daughter of his king. Frequently the king admonishes him: 'You have done this and that.' The nobleman asks the courtiers: 'Who among you has informed against me?' They laugh at him, 'Are you not wedded to the royal princess?' By the same token, man is wedded to the soul, who is the daughter of God and informs Him of all secret deeds."

JUDAISM: PESIKTA RABBATI, 8:2

When God sends down His daughter, the pure soul, to labor in this world within the body, let us pray that we may return her to her Father, when her time is over, free from sin.

JUDAISM: ZOHAR, III, 97A

You won't see signs of the coming of the kingdom of God. It won't be a matter of saying "Here it is!" or "There!" Look – the kingdom of God is within you.

CHRISTIANITY: LUKE 17.20–1

Do you not know that you are God's temple and that God's Spirit dwells in you? For God's temple is holy, and you are that temple.

CHRISTIANITY: 1 CORINTHIANS 3.16–17

I was a secret treasure, and I created the creatures in order that I might be known.

ISLAM: HADITH

God is not far from each one of us, for "In him we live and move and have our being."

CHRISTIANITY: ACTS 17.27–8

We indeed created man; and We know what his soul whispers within him, and We are nearer to him than the jugular vein.

ISLAM: QUR'AN 50.16

When I love him, I am his hearing by which he hears; and his sight by which he sees; his hand by which he strikes; and his foot by which he walks.

ISLAM: FORTY HADITH OF AN-NAWAWI 38

Ever is He present with you – think not He is far: By the Master's teaching recognize Him within yourself.

SIKHISM: ADI GRANTH, MAJH ASHTPADI M.3

LEFT
Miniature showing Jesus fleeing Damascus with two angels, Turkish, 16th century.

UNION WITH GOD

Above the doorway into the ancient pagan sanctuary of Apollo were written the words "Know Your Self." Self-knowledge was the supreme goal of the mystery religions. Through their sacred rites, the ancients sought knowledge of the soul and union with God. Mystery initiation rituals were a profound secret that was never openly divulged. We know from the Egyptian sage Plotinus (205–270 C.E.), however, that an initiate moved beyond the statues and representations of the gods and, in the inner sanctuary, directly experienced a transcendental vision.

Plotinus pictures the soul as a circle with God as the still center. The aim of the initiate is to live in perfect harmony with this center and so become a god himself. Just as two circles which share the same center point become indistinguishable, the initiate experiences the Self as identical with God. In this knowledge of oneness there is no duality, so there is no separation between God and soul. God is no longer other, but one's very Self.

The soul moves naturally in a circle
around an inner center,
which is the point from which the circle issues.
To be bound to that center is to be a god.
To be apart from it is to be a complex, animal man.

We always revolve about the One,
but we do not always pay attention to it.
Like a chorus singing harmoniously around its conductor
becomes discordant when it turns away from him,
but sings beautifully when turned inward and fully attentive –
we similarly revolve around the Oneness of God,
but do not always look to him.
Yet when we do, we find our home and resting place.
Around him we dance the true dance;
God-inspired and no longer dissonant.

In that moment of vision,
the Self into which we merge is perceived as simple unity.
It is better not to talk of what sees, but of what is seen.
Bolder still – abandon altogether the duality of seer and seen.
Count both as one,
for in that vision the seer does not experience "two."
He is changed.
He is no longer himself.
Nor does he own himself,
but belongs to God.
He is One with him – center joined with center.

When centers coincide, they are one.
When parted there are two.
This is why in our present state we speak of God as "other."
But in contemplation what is seen cannot be described.
What "other" is there to report,
when what is seen is not separate,
but one with our Self?

As if carried away or possessed by a god,
we have found the solitude of untroubled stillness.
Our being is not distracted or busied with our personal self,
but is completely at rest.
We have gone beyond what is beautiful,
leaving behind even the choir of virtues.
We are like someone who enters the inner sanctuary,
passing beyond the temple statues.
We don't converse with any mere representation,
but with Godhead itself.
And this is not something seen,
but another way of seeing –
a detachment from the personal self,
a simplification and surrender, a longing for contact,
a tranquil meditation allowing transformation.
Only in this way may someone know
what lies within the sanctuary.
For someone who looks in any other way,
there is nothing to be seen.

ANCIENT MYSTERY RELIGIONS: PLOTINUS X, MYSTICAL UNION

ABOVE
The Temple of Apollo
Epikourios, Bassae,
1854-55
by Edward Lear
(1812-88).

TRANSCENDING THE EGO

The Zen Buddhist master Hashida writes, "To study the way of the Buddha is to study your own self. To study your self is to forget yourself." This statement captures the paradox found in many scriptures. The essential Self is divine and eternal, but through identifying itself with a mortal body and personality, it ceases to be aware of its true nature. The personal ego-self obscures the true Self. This is the cause of human suffering. Our word *personality* comes from the Greek term *persona* meaning "mask." The personality is a mask worn by the true Self. It is who we think we are. But it is only an idea, an illusion. To find what we actually are, we must see beyond the mask of what we take ourselves to be. To know the One, we must transcend the ego which creates our sense of separateness from God.

The thought of "I" in what is not the Self brings the Spirit into bondage. This bondage, springing from unwisdom, brings on us birth and death and weariness. He who identifies himself with his body thinks the unenduring is real, and therefore feeds it, anoints it, guards it, and so is enmeshed in the things of sense like a silkworm in the threads it spins.

He who is subject to this illusion suffers many sorrows. To take the unreal for the real is bondage. Friend, heed this.

When the stainless, radiant, true Self is concealed, the deluded man thinks of the body, which is not the Self, as "I." Then the far-reaching power of desire causes disintegration, painfully binding him with the cords of lust and anger.

As a wreath of cloud is brought into being by the sun's shining, yet spreads and conceals the sun, so the personal self, which comes into being through the Self, spreads and conceals the true Self.

LEFT
Wall painting of the Vairochana Buddha, Balawaste, 7th-8th century.

Just as in bad weather the lord of day is swallowed up by heavy clouds and fierce blasts of cold wind, so when the true Self is enveloped by unbroken darkness, the power of disintegration brings the deluded man much suffering.

This bondage to that which is not Self, which has its root in unwisdom, arises without a cause. It is beginningless and endless, bringing upon the separate self a flood of sorrows, such as birth and death, sickness and decay.

HINDUISM: SANKARA, THE CREST JEWEL OF WISDOM

Where egoism exists,
You are not experienced.
Where You are, there is no ego.
Learned people,
expound in your mind
this inexpressible proposition.

SIKHISM: ADI GRANTH, MARU-KI-VAR M.1

O Son of Man! If you love Me, turn
away from yourself; and if you seek
My pleasure, regard not your own;
that you may die in Me and I may
eternally live in you.

BAHA'I FAITH: HIDDEN WORDS OF
BAHA'U'LLAH, ARABIC 7

I have been crucified with Christ;
it is no longer I who live,
but Christ who lives in me.

CHRISTIANITY: GALATIANS 2.20

Torah abides only with him who
regards himself as nothing.

JUDAISM: TALMUD, SOTA 21B

My spirit was carried to heaven.
It looked at nothing
although Paradise and Hell
were displayed before it,
for it was free from the veils of phenomena.
I became a bird,
with a body of Oneness and wings of Eternity,
flying in the air of the Absolute,
until I passed through Purification,
and gazed upon the meadow of Eternity
and saw there the tree of Oneness.
When I looked at myself, I was these things.
I cried out : "O Lord,
with my ego I cannot attain You,
yet I cannot escape from my separate self.
What can I do?"
God said: "Win freedom from your you-ness
through my Beloved Muhammad.
Smear your eyes with dust from his feet
and follow him continually."

ISLAM: SUFI MASTER BAYAZID OF BISTAMI

THE WITNESS

According to the mystical traditions of all religions, when human beings relinquish their sense of being merely a body and personality, they discover that their essential nature is Pure Consciousness, the eternal witness of all actions and thoughts. This idea is particularly clear in Eastern scriptures, which call this supreme spiritual realization *enlightenment*.

The Buddha was asked if an enlightened being could be said to still exist. He replied, "You could not say he does, but you could not say he does not." Such a one is beyond description. When the self is realized as the eternal witness, there is no one to die, for no one was born. There is no one to exist or not exist. There is simply permanent immortal consciousness witnessing the continually unfolding changes of life.

The external world is then seen to be a projection of the Self, an illusion which the Indians call *samsara*. Everything is the Atman, the Self. This sublime realization is attained when all ideas of me and mine are given up. For an enlightened being, there is no division between self and other. There is no duality at all. Even samsara and nirvana, the illusion of the world and Pure Consciousness, are not separate at all. They exist because of each other and can not be divided. The experience (samsara) exists because there is an experiencer (nirvana) and the experiencer exists because there is an experience. The seer and the seen are indivisibly one. Everything is one.

You are neither earth, nor water, nor fire, nor air, nor space. You are the witness of those elements as Consciousness. Understanding this is liberation.

If you detach yourself from identification with the body and remain relaxed in and as Consciousness, you will, this very moment, be happy, at peace, free from bondage.

You have been bitten by the deadly black serpent of the ego and you therefore consider yourself as the doer. Drink the nectar of the faith that you are not the doer and be happy.

You are that Consciousness – Supreme Bliss – upon which appears this phenomenal manifestation, like the illusion of a snake on a rope. Live happily.

The Atman is the sole witness, all pervading, perfect, free Consciousness – actionless, unattached, desireless, at peace with itself. It is only through an illusion that it appears to be involved with the samsara.

Give up the illusion that you are the individual self together with all external and internal self-modifications, and meditate on the Atman, the immutable, non-dual Consciousness.

It is you that pervades this universe, and this universe exists in you. You are truly pure Consciousness by nature. Be not petty-minded. Just as the surface of a mirror exists within and without the image reflected in the mirror, so also the supreme Self exists both within and without the physical body.

HINDUISM: ASHTAVAKRA GITA 2–19

Shun ill pride and jealousy. Give up all idea of "me" and "mine." As long as there is consciousness of diversity and not of unity in the Self, a man ignorantly thinks of himself as a separate being, as the "doer" of actions and the "experiencer" of effects. He remains subject to birth and death, knows happiness and misery, is bound by his own deeds, good or bad.

HINDUISM: SRIMAD BHAGAVATAM 11.4

BELOW
Banner showing the Buddha preaching, Chinese, 8th century.

Where one sees nothing but the One, hears nothing but the One, knows nothing but the One – there is the Infinite. Where one sees another, hears another, knows another – there is the finite. The Infinite is immortal, the finite is mortal. It is written, He who has realized eternal Truth does not see death, nor illness, nor pain; he sees everything as the Self, and obtains all.

HINDUISM: CHANDOGYA UPANISHAD 7.23
AND 7.27

When a man is free from all sense pleasures and depends on nothingness, he is free in the supreme freedom from perception. He will stay there and not return again. It is like a flame struck by a sudden gust of wind. In a flash it has gone out and nothing more can be known about it. It is the same with a wise man freed from mental existence: In a flash he has gone out and nothing more can be known about him. When a person has gone out, then there is nothing by which you can measure him. That by which he can be talked about is no longer there for him; yet you cannot say that he does not exist. When all ways of being, all phenomena are removed, then all ways of description have also been removed.

BUDDHISM: SUTTA NIPATA 1072–6

CHAPTER THREE

The Spiritual Path

WHAT IS THE PURPOSE of human life? The scriptures answer that, above all, we are here to walk the spiritual path. Although different traditions describe the spiritual path in different ways, there are recurring common themes. The spiritual path is a search for experiential knowledge of the Truth. It is an attempt to live a good life in harmony with divine laws. It is opening the heart to an all-embracing love. It is devoting one's actions to the unselfish service of others. It is worship and devotion. It is surrendering one's personal will to the divine will. It is a preparation for the challenge of facing the mystery of death and the life beyond. It is the path to becoming enlightened.

This chapter explores the idea of life as a pilgrimage towards spiritual awakening. Central to this adventure is cultivating the remembrance of God through prayer and meditation, so that our lives are subsumed by the spiritual quest. Although this path requires individual effort, many traditions point to the intervention of God's grace as the real source of spiritual illumination.

To become aware of the eternal oneness, we must cease to be attached to the transitory things of life. To cultivate detachment, sects in all religions have practiced forms of asceticism, attempting to become full of spirit by rejecting the world. The Buddha, however, having experienced extremes of both wealth and self-imposed destitution, teaches the Middle Way, which leads to the end of suffering and the attainment of enlightenment.

At the end of the spiritual journey lies a mystical paradox. For an enlightened being there is in reality nowhere to go and no spiritual path to follow. Everything is already perfect and has been all along. The spiritual journey leads to the realization that we are already where we need to be. We are now, and always have been, part of the one. All that has changed is our understanding. Nothing is different, and yet everything is different. Heaven has always been laid out before us, but only now do we see it.

OPPOSITE
Illumination showing the sacrifice of Isaac.

BER · GENERATIONIS

BECOMING A SPIRITUAL PILGRIM

The spiritual path is a search for our self. It cannot be walked for us by anyone else. It is the expansion of our own awareness, which cannot be had by proxy. It is a personal adventure into consciousness. According to Islamic scripture, we are here to fight the supreme *jihad* – a holy war, not against others, but against our own lower nature which separates us from God. All that is required of us is to commit ourselves fully to the challenge and to ask for God's help. As a Nigerian Igbo wisdom proverb puts it, "If you say yes, your God will say yes."

*What the superior man seeks
is in himself,
what the lesser man seeks is in others.*

CONFUCIANISM: ANALECTS 15.20

PICTURES THIS
PAGE
*Abraham and the
sacrifice of Isaac,
Anglo-Saxon.*

*If I am not for myself who is for me?
And when I am for myself
what am I?
And if not now, when?*

JUDAISM: ABOT 1.14

Ask, and it will be given to you; seek, and you will find; knock, and it will be opened to you. For every one who asks receives, and he who seeks finds, and to him who knocks it will be opened.

For who of you, if his son asks him for bread, will give him a stone? Or if he asks for fish, will give him a serpent? If you, then, who are imperfect, know how to give good gifts to your children, how much more will your Father who is in heaven give good things to those who ask him!

CHRISTIANITY: MATTHEW 7.7–11

*Work out your own salvation
with fear and trembling.*

CHRISTIANITY: PHILIPPIANS 2.12

*Jesus said "Let him who seeks
continue seeking until he finds. When
he finds, he will become troubled.
When he becomes troubled, he will be
astonished, and will rule over the all."*

CHRISTIANITY: THE GNOSTIC GOSPEL OF

THOMAS 2

*O believers! You have charge over your own souls.
God changes not what is in a people, until they change what is in themselves.*

ISLAM: QUR'AN 5.105 AND 13.11

*The Prophet declared, "We have returned from the lesser holy war (at jihad al-asghar) to the greater holy war (at jihad al-akbar)."
They asked, "O Prophet of God, which is the greater war?" He replied, "Struggle against the lower self."*

ISLAM: HADITH

*The Master said: There is one thing in this world which must never be forgotten. If you were to forget everything else, but did not forget that, then there would be no cause to worry; whereas if you performed and remembered and did not forget every single thing, but forgot that one thing, then you would have done nothing whatsoever.
It is just as if a king had sent you to the country to carry out a specified task. You go and perform a hundred other tasks; but if you have not performed that particular task on account of which you had gone to the country, it is as though you have performed nothing at all. So man has come into this world for a particular task, and that is his purpose; if he does not perform it, then he will have done nothing.*

ISLAM: DISCOURSES OF RUMI 4

BELOW
An angel brings a ram as Abraham is about to sacrifice Isaac, Turkish, 1583.

REMEMBERING GOD

Scripture urges the remembrance of God as a fundamental part of the spiritual path. The pagan initiate Iamblichus (c.230–325 C.E.) extols the power of prayer. The Islamic Hadith teaches that Allah is with us whenever we put our thoughts on him. Jewish scripture urges silent communion. The ancient Zoroastrian Avesta praises pondering the acts of holy men. The Sikh Adi Granath counsels contemplation as the way to peace of body and mind. The Hindu Svetasvatara Upanishad suggests meditation as a way to cultivate an awareness of our unity with the Divine. The Isha Upanishad, however, cautions against getting lost in the inner world as well as in the outer world and recommends a balanced life of action and meditation.

Since prayers are by no means the last part of sacrifice, but instead contribute something that is essential to its completion and thus supply to the whole rite its power and its effect, and since, moreover they serve to enhance the general reverence for God and create a sacred, indissoluble bond of fellowship with the gods, it seems not inappropriate to say a few words upon the subject. Moreover it is a subject that is worth knowing about in and for itself; further, it completes our knowledge of the gods. I therefore affirm that the first kind of prayer is that which brings God and man together. Since it brings about the association with the divine and gives us the knowledge thereof. The second establishes a bond of fellowship founded upon like-mindedness and calls down gifts sent by the gods, which arrive before we can ask for them and perfect our efforts even without our knowledge. The third and most perfect form finally seals the secret union, which

hands over every decision privately to the gods and leaves our souls completely at rest in them.

No sacred act can be effective without the supplication of prayer. Steady continuance in prayer nourishes our mind, enlarges the soul for the reception of the gods, opens up to men the realm of the gods, accustoms us to the splendor of the divine light, and gradually perfects in us our union with the gods, until at last it leads us back to the supreme heights. Our mode of thinking is drawn gently aloft and implants in us the spirit of the gods; it awakens confidence, fellowship, and undying friendship with them; it increases the longing for God ; it inflames in us whatever is divine within the soul; it banishes all opposition from the soul, and strips away from the radiant, light-formed spirit everything that leads to generation; it creates good hope and trust in the light. In brief, it gives to those who engage in it intercourse with the gods.

ANCIENT MYSTERY RELIGIONS: IAMBLICHUS, ON THE MYSTERIES

ABOVE
Portrait of Iamblichus from Jacques Bossard's De Devinatione et Magicis.

On You alone we ever meditate,
And ponder over the teachings of the
Loving Mind,
As well as the acts of the holy men,
Whose souls accord most perfectly
with Truth.

ZOROASTRIANISM: AVESTA, YASNA 34.2

Commune with your own heart
upon your bed,
and be silent.

JUDAISM AND CHRISTIANITY: PSALM 4.4

You keep him in perfect peace,
whose mind is stayed on You,
because he trusts in You.

JUDAISM AND CHRISTIANITY: ISAIAH 26.3

For everything there is an
appropriate way of polishing; the
heart's polishing is the remembrance
of God.

ISLAM: HADITH OF TIRMIDHI

In the dark night live those for whom
the world without alone is real; in
night darker still live those for whom
the world within alone is real. The
first leads to a life of action, the
second to a life of meditation. But
those who combine action with
meditation cross the sea of death
through action and enter into
immortality through the practice of
meditation. So have we heard from
the wise.

HINDUISM: ISHA UPANISHAD 9–11

God has declared: I am close to the
thought that My servant has of Me,
and I am with him whenever he
recollects Me. If he remembers Me in
himself, I remember him in Myself,
and if he remembers Me in a
gathering I remember him better
than those in the gathering do, and if
he approaches Me by as much as one
hand's length, I approach him by a
cubit. If he takes a step towards Me, I
run towards him.

ISLAM: HADITH

Should anyone be victim
of great anxiety,
his body racked with maladies,
beset with problems
of home and family,
with pleasure and pain alternating,
wandering in all four directions
without peace or rest;
should he then contemplate
the Supreme Being,
peaceful shall his mind
and body become.

SIKHISM: ADI GRANTH, SRI RAGA M.5

Meditate upon him and transcend
physical consciousness. Thus will you
reach union with the Lord of the
universe. Thus will you become
identified with him who is One
without a second. In him all your
desires will find fulfillment. The truth
is that you are always united with the
Lord. But you must know this.

HINDUISM: SVETASVATARA UPANISHAD
1.11–12

ABOVE
Illumination of
"Blessed are the poor
in spirit," English,
c. 1870.

NON-ATTACHMENT

Scripture advises us to be unattached to the transitory things of life, such as wealth, success, and even our own body and loved ones. By their very nature all of these things must pass away, and we must accept their passing with equanimity. We must learn to be in the world but not of it. By developing the quality of detachment, we give up the impossible struggle to find permanence in an ever-changing world and can begin to focus instead on the permanent immortal Self within.

The craziness that results from our attachments to the impermanent things of life is brought out in a charming allegory in the Buddhist Yogacara Bhumi Sutra. The desire of the ego-self to control the world is like a child building sand-castles, and the conflicts which result are just as ridiculous. Things which the personality fights to protect are known to be of absolutely no value by the enlightened sage, who has returned to the oneness of his eternal home.

Some children were playing beside a river. They made castles of sand, and each child defended his castle and said, "This one is mine." They kept their castles separate and would not allow any mistakes about which was whose. When the castles were all finished, one child kicked over someone else's castle and completely destroyed it. The owner of the castle flew into a rage, pulled the other child's hair, struck him with his fist and bawled out, "He has spoiled my castle! Come along all of you and help me to punish him as he deserves." The others all came to his help. They beat the child with a stick and then stamped on him as he lay on the ground. Then they went on playing in their sand castles, each saying, "This is mine; no one else may have it. Keep away! Don't touch my castle!" But evening came, it was getting dark and they all thought they ought to be going home. No one now cared what became of his castle. One child stamped on his, another pushed his over with both hands. Then they turned away and went back, each to his home.

BUDDHISM: YOGACARA BHUMI SUTRA 4

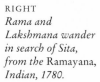

RIGHT
Rama and Lakshmana wander in search of Sita, from the Ramayana, *Indian, 1780.*

Be in the world as if you were a stranger or a traveler.

ISLAM: FORTY HADITH OF AN-NAVAWI 40

Jesus said: "Become a passer-by."

CHRISTIANITY: GOSPEL OF THOMAS 44

ASCETICISM

Most religions have sects which have seen asceticism as a way of exiling the world, by denying its pleasures, and so coming to know God. This was a path adopted by the fifth-century B.C.E. Indian sage Gautama, who is known by the title Buddha which means "Knower" or "Enlightened One." He is said to have been born a prince and lived a life of luxury. It had been prophesied at his birth that Gautama would become either a great worldly man or a great spiritual being. His father shielded him completely from the sufferings of the world in an attempt to forestall any spiritual leanings, but Gautama discovered the awful realities of illness, grief, old age, and death when he convinced his chariot driver to drive him through the city. He then set out on a search for meaning and became a strict ascetic. Only when he stopped his self-torture, however, did he finally experience enlightenment and became the Tathagata, "he who has fully arrived."

To such a pitch of asceticism have I gone that naked was I, flouting life's decencies, licking my hands after meals, never heeding when folk called to me to come or to stop. I have lived on a single saucer of food a day. My sole diet has been herbs gathered green, or the discarded scum of rice on the boil, or cow-dung. My raiment has been of hemp or of rags from the dust-heap, of grass, of strips of bark or wood, of hair of men or animals woven into a blanket or of owl's wings. In fulfillment of my vows, I have plucked out the hair of my head and the hair of my beard.

In a charnel ground I lay me down with charred bones for pillow. When the cowherds' boys came along, they spat and urinated upon me, pelted me with dirt and stuck bits of wood into my ears. Yet I declare that never did I let an evil mood against them arise within me – so poised in equanimity was I.

My body grew emaciated in the extreme; because I ate so little, my members, great and small, grew like the knotted joints of withered creepers; like a buffalo's hoof were my shrunken buttocks; like the twists in a rope were my spinal vertebrae; like the crazy rafters of a tumble-down roof were my gaunt ribs; like the starry gleams on water deep down and afar in the depths of a well, shone my gleaming eyes deep down and afar in the depths of their sockets; and as the rind of a cut gourd shrinks and shrivels in the heat, so shrank and shriveled the scalp of my head – and all because I ate so little.

Never did this practice or these courses or these dire austerities bring me to the ennobling gifts of super-human knowledge and insight. And why? Because none of them leads to that noble understanding which, when won, leads on to Deliverance and guides him who lives up to it onward to the utter extinction of all suffering.

BUDDHISM: MAJJHIMA-NIKAYA XII MAHA-SIHANADA-SUTTA

BELOW
Fresco showing St. Benedict and his friars begging, by Sodoma (Vercelli) (1477-1549).

THE MIDDLE WAY

In the Mahavagga, the Buddha advises his monks, called *Bhikkhus*, to follow the Middle Way. He teaches the famous Eight Fold Path and the Four Noble Truths. The essence of the Buddha's teachings is this: Human beings are enmeshed in suffering. If we don't have what we want, we suffer. If we have what we don't want, we suffer. If we have what we want, we know that eventually we must lose it, and so we suffer. Suffering is caused by the desire for things to be other than they are. Extinguishing desire leads to the end of suffering and the beginning of enlightenment. When the venerable Kondanna heard the Buddha's words, he was illuminated by understanding the simple fact that everything that comes into being must also pass away and that trying to hold onto the transitory only brings suffering.

ABOVE
A Buddhist in meditation.

"There are two extremes, O Bhikkhus, which he who has given up the world, ought to avoid. What are these two extremes? A life devoted to pleasures and lusts: this is degrading, sensual, vulgar, ignoble, and profitless; and a life given to mortifications: this is painful, ignoble, and profitless. By avoiding these two extremes, O Bhikkhus, the Tathagata has gained the knowledge of the Middle Path which leads to insight, which leads to wisdom, which conduces to calm, to knowledge, to Nirvana.

"Which, O Bhikkhus, is this Middle Path? It is the holy eightfold Path, namely, Right Belief, Right Aspiration, Right Speech, Right Conduct, Right Means of Livelihood, Right Endeavor, Right Memory, Right Meditation. This, O Bhikkhus, is the Middle Path the knowledge of which the Tathagata has gained, which leads to insight, which leads to wisdom, which conduces to calm, to knowledge, to Nirvana.

"This, O Bhikkhus, is the Noble Truth of Suffering: Birth is suffering: decay is suffering; illness is suffering; death is suffering. Presence of objects we hate is suffering; Separation from objects we love is suffering; not to obtain what we desire is suffering. Briefly, the fivefold clinging to existence is suffering.

"This, O Bhikkhus, is the Noble Truth of the Cause of suffering: Thirst, that leads to re-birth, accompanied by pleasure and lust, finding its delight here and there. This thirst is threefold, namely, thirst for pleasure, thirst for existence, thirst for prosperity.

"This, O Bhikkhus, is the Noble Truth of the Cessation of suffering: it ceases with the complete cessation of this thirst – a cessation which consists in the absence of every passion – with the abandoning of this thirst, with the doing away with it, with the deliverance from it, with the destruction of desire.

"This, O Bhikkhus, is the Noble Truth of the Path which leads to the cessation of suffering: that holy eightfold Path, that is to say, Right Belief, Right Aspiration, Right Speech, Right Conduct, Right Means of Livelihood, Right Endeavor, Right Memory, Right Meditation."

This is what the Blessed One said. The five Bhikkhus were delighted, and they rejoiced at the words of the Blessed One. And when this teaching was propounded, the venerable Kondanna obtained the pure and spotless Eye of the Truth – that is to say, the following knowledge: Whatsoever is subject to the condition of origination, is subject also to the condition of cessation.

BUDDHISM: MAHAVAGGA I, 6, 17–30

LIBERATION

The end of the spiritual journey is direct knowledge of God. The joy, ecstasy, gratitude, and sense of liberation which this experience evokes is beautifully conveyed by some of the Odes of Solomon. Five of these odes are contained in a Gnostic Christian text called Pistis Sophia. In 1909 a complete collection of Syriac odes was discovered in a Jewish hymnbook. They are attributed to the great Jewish sage King Solomon. Some believe they indeed have a Jewish origin, others that they are part of a Gnostic Christian hymnal. They are certainly quoted by the early Christian Church Fathers. They have a profound haunting quality and are some of the most beautiful sacred poems of antiquity.

I was freed from myself
and uncondemned.
The chain fell from my wrists.

I took on the face and ways
of a new person,
walked in him and was redeemed.

The thought of truth drove me.
I walked to it
and did not wander off.

Those who saw me were amazed,
supposing me to be a strange person.

He who knew me and brought me up
is the summit of perfection.

He glorified me by kindness
and lifted my thought to truth

and showed me his way.
I opened closed doors,

shattered bars of iron.
My own shackles melted.

Nothing appeared closed
because I was the door to everything.

I freed slaves,
left no man in bonds,

I spread my knowledge
and love

and sowed my fruits in hearts
and transformed them.

I blessed them. They lived.
I gathered them and saved them.

They became the limbs of my body
and I was their head.

Glory to you, our head,
our Lord Messiah.

JUDAISM AND CHRISTIANITY: ODES OF
SOLOMON 17

Effort and grace

Different traditions within each religion emphasize either the need to rely on one's own personal effort or the intervention of divine grace. This apparent dichotomy is clearly illustrated by Buddhist scripture. The Buddha teaches his followers to seek their own enlightenment, as he himself had done, not relying on external help. The meditation school known as Zen urges self-reliance to the point of seeing holy scripture as waste paper, for books are only full of concepts which get in the way of the student's directly perceiving the truth. Veneration of Zen masters, and even of the Buddha himself, is seen as a potential impediment to the student's own enlightenment, for to see Buddha as someone outside of the Self is to miss the whole point.

The Pure Land Buddhist sect takes an opposite approach. It sees spiritual liberation as only possible through the intervention of celestial godlike Buddhas such as Amida Buddha. These Buddhists seek to be reborn after death in the heavenly Pure Lands, in which conditions are more conducive to the attainment of enlightenment than here. Shinran (1173–1262) is the founder of one of the most important of Pure Land sects. He teaches that it is easier for a wicked man who knows he cannot achieve illumination for himself to be reborn in the Pure Lands, than it is for a good man who trusts in his own power. He recommends abandoning reliance on our own power altogether and having faith in the Power of Another – totally trusting in Amida Buddha's vow to rescue beings from the sufferings of this life.

The paradox underlying these two positions is this: if the seeker relies on the grace of a deity to enlighten him, the seeker is merely projecting the self onto something external, making it harder to find. But relying on the effort generated by his own ego-self in order to overcome his own ego-self is like trying to pull himself up by his own bootstraps. It won't work. It merely endorses the illusion of being a separate self.

There is no real dichotomy here, however. Any spiritual practice is actually only laying the conditions which may allow a spontaneous realization that can never be forced or demanded, and any celestial deities called on for help are actually a device to trick the ego into giving up its claims to personal power. When enlightenment occurs naturally, the seeker will find both celestial Buddhas and the ego-self to have been illusions.

Most spiritual traditions teach a combination of personal effort and relying on God's grace. From an enlightened perspective the irony is that the two are indistinguishable. Any effort we may think we are making is in fact God's grace, and any grace that we believe to be coming from an external source is in reality coming from the true Self.

"*If even a good man can be reborn in the Pure Land, how much more so a wicked man.*" *People generally think, however, that if even a wicked man can be reborn in the Pure Land, how much more so a good man! This latter view may at first sight seem reasonable, but it is not in accord with the purpose of the Original Vow, with faith in the Power of Another. The reason for this is that he who, relying on his own power, undertakes to perform meritorious deeds, has no intention of relying on the Power of Another and is not the object of the Original Vow of Amida. Should he, however, abandon his reliance on his own power and put his trust in the Power of Another, he can be born in the True Land of Recompense.*

We who are caught in the net of our own passions cannot free ourselves from bondage to birth and death, no matter what kind of austerities or good deeds we try to perform. Seeing this and pitying our condition, Amida made his Vow with the intention of bringing wicked men to Buddhahood. Therefore the wicked man who depends on the Power of Another is the prime object of salvation. This is the reason why Shinran said, "If even a good man can be reborn in the Pure Land, how much more so a wicked man!"

BUDDHISM: THE SAYINGS OF SHINRAN

BELOW
Lao Tzu, the legendary founder of Taoism, by Qian Gu, 16th century.

*You are the lamp
To lighten the way.
Then hurry, hurry.*

*When your light shines purely
You will not be born
And you will not die.*

BUDDHISM: DHAMMAPADA 18

"*Please, Man of Shakya,*" *said Dhotaka, "free me from confusion!" "It is not in my practice to free anyone from confusion," said the Buddha. "When you have understood the most valuable teachings, then you yourself will cross this ocean."*

BUDDHISM: SUTTA NIPATA 1063–4

You must be lamps unto yourselves. Rely on yourselves, and do not rely on external help. Hold firm to the truth as a lamp and a refuge, and do not look for refuge to anything besides yourselves. A brother becomes his own lamp and refuge by continually looking on his body, feelings, perceptions, moods, and ideas in such a manner that he conquers the cravings and depressions of ordinary men and is always strenuous, self-possessed, and collected in mind. Whoever among my disciples does this, either now or when I am dead, if he is anxious to learn, will reach the summit.

BUDDHISM: DIGHA NIKAYA II.99–100,
MAHAPARINIBBANA SUTTANTA

THE ROAD TO NOWHERE

From the point of view of an enlightened being, the spiritual path itself is seen ultimately to be an illusion. He has become aware that everything is one and always has been. There never was anywhere to go, or anyone to go there. The Taoist sage Chuang Tzu paints a picture of a natural human being in harmony with the oneness of Tao. He does not distinguish himself from the rest of life. He does not even have a name. When asked how to bring peace to the world he is dismissive and unconcerned. For such a being the world is already at peace. In the Gnostic Gospel of Thomas, Jesus likewise tells his disciples that heaven is already here for those with eyes to see it.

The limitation inherent in the idea of a spiritual path is illustrated by the Buddhist Sutra of Hui Neng. Hui Neng was a Chinese sage of the Chan school, more familiar by its Japanese name, Zen. The sutra relates that the fifth Zen patriarch was looking for a successor and decided to test the level of insight of his students by asking them to submit a poem to him. Most of the monks assumed that this honor would go to a learned monk called Shen Hsiu. In his poem Shen Hsiu compared the body to the tree of knowledge and the mind to a mirror in need of cleaning through persistent spiritual practice. The master understood from this that Shen Hsiu's insight was limited, for he still thought that there was something to attain and someone to attain it. Hui Neng was at this time an illiterate kitchen worker. Yet he understood that everything is void, since separate things have no existence independent of the oneness, and so there is no impure personal mind in need of purification. Hui Neng takes up the story...

BELOW
Detail from the Diamond Sutra.

I, Hui Neng, was pounding rice when I heard a young boy reciting the stanza written by Shen Hsiu.
Our body is the Bodhi tree,
And our mind a mirror bright,
Carefully we wipe them hour by hour,
And let no dust alight.
I dictated my stanza, which read,
There is no Bodhi tree,
Nor any mirror bright.
Since all is void,
Where can the dust alight?
When this had been written, the crowd of disciples was overwhelmed with amazement, but the Patriarch rubbed off the stanza with his shoe, lest jealous ones should do me injury. The next night he invited me secretly to his room, and expounded the Diamond Sutra to me. When he came to the sentence, "One should use one's mind in such a way that it will be free from any attachment," I at

once became thoroughly enlightened, and realized that all things in the universe are the Essence of Mind itself. "Who would have thought," I said to the Patriarch, "that the Essence of Mind is intrinsically pure!" Thus, to the knowledge of no one, the Dharma was transmitted to me at midnight, and I became the Sixth Patriarch.

BUDDHISM: SUTRA OF HUI NENG 1

T'ien Ken was traveling to the south of Yin Mountain. He had reached the river Liao when he met a nameless sage, to whom he said, "I beg to ask about governing the world."

"Go away," said the nameless man, "you are a low fellow. How unpleasant is your question! I would be in companionship with the Maker of things. When wearied, I would mount on the bird of ease and emptiness, proceed beyond the world, wander in the land of nowhere, and live in the domain of nothingness. Why do you come to worry me with the problem of setting the world in order?"

T'ien Ken again asked his question, and the nameless man replied: "Make excursion in pure simplicity. Identify yourself with non-distinction. Follow the nature of things and admit no personal bias, then the world will be in peace."

TAOISM: CHUANG TZU

His disciples said to him "When will the kingdom come?" Jesus said "It will not come by waiting for it. It will not be a matter of saying 'here it is' or 'there it is.' Rather the kingdom of the father is spread out upon the earth and men do not see it."

CHRISTIANITY: THE
GOSPEL OF THOMAS 111

BELOW
Dreaming of
Immortality in a
Thatched Cottage,
*T'ang Yin
(1470-1523).*

CHAPTER FOUR

Knowledge and Wisdom

MODERN SCIENCE HAS often criticized religion for encouraging blind faith. Actually, however, the spiritual path leads beyond belief to experiential knowledge. Ancient pagans and early Gnostic Christians experienced *gnosis*, which is Greek for "knowledge," and called an initiate a Gnostic or Knower. Buddhists aspire to become a Buddha, which also means Knower. The Buddha, however, is not a person who knows something which we do not. The Buddha is the consciousness inside each one of us that does the knowing. To become a Gnostic or Buddha we must know the knower within ourselves.

The Hindus call their oldest scriptures *Vedas* which means "knowledge" and their sages *gnanis* meaning "knowers." The Gnani path is one of the traditional spiritual paths a Hindu may travel towards liberation. It is the path of using the mind to go beyond the mind. Ideas are not able to contain the truth but are more like windows through which the nature of reality may be glimpsed. A clear idea is one that you can clearly see through.

The scriptures are a sacred source of such transcendental ideas. The knowledge which they impart is not a collection of facts. Ultimately, it is a direct and nonconceptual knowledge of God. We talk about knowing someone in the biblical sense because in the Bible the word *know* is also used to signify sexual intercourse, in which two people become one. In the experience of spiritual knowledge, the knower becomes one with the known. The spiritual pilgrim does not know about God; he or she is one with God. Teachings and doctrines may be a way to this knowledge, but they are not the knowledge. They are, to use an image from Zen Buddhism, a finger pointing at the moon but not the moon itself.

OPPOSITE
Detail from the Book of St. Medard of Soissons, *French, early 9th century.*

THE SEARCH FOR KNOWLEDGE

Spiritual knowledge, sometimes called wisdom or understanding, is praised by all religious traditions. Christian and Hindu scriptures honor knowledge for its power to set us free. For Buddhists, knowledge is the chief faculty of mind helpful to enlightenment. Jewish scripture says, "The spirit became pregnant and brought forth wisdom" (Shemat Rabbah 1 15:22). Spiritual knowledge is the child of the love affair between a human being and God.

He who has understanding has everything.

JUDAISM: NEDARIM 41

You will know the truth, and the truth will make you free.

CHRISTIANITY: JOHN 8.32

Seek not for life on earth or in heaven. Thirst for life is delusion. Knowing life to be transitory, wake up from this dream of ignorance and strive to attain knowledge and freedom.

HINDUISM: SRIMAD BHAGAVATAM 11.13

Just as there is no cooking without fire, so freedom cannot be accomplished without wisdom.

HINDUISM: SANKARA, ATMA BOHDA 2

As the lion, the king of the beasts, is recognized chief among animals, for his strength, speed, and bravery, so is the faculty of wisdom reckoned chief among mental states helpful to enlightenment. And what are the mental states helpful to enlightenment? The faculty of faith, of vigor, of mindfulness, of concentration, of wisdom: each conduces to enlightenment.

BUDDHISM: SAMYUTTA-NIKAYA V, 227

BELOW
The Reading of the Bible by the Rabbis, *J. A. Lecomte de Nouy, 19th century.*

KNOWLEDGE BEYOND CONCEPTS

Jain scripture compares religious doctrines to sea water contained in a pot. It is water from the sea, but it is not the ocean. In the same way religious doctrines are and are not the truth. All concepts, no matter how sublime, are by their very nature limited and limiting. God must always be too great to be contained by them. Ideas may be helpful on the spiritual journey, but ultimately the mystical traditions within every religion see them as obstacles to true knowledge. They are a wire mesh through which we perceive reality. To see the undistorted truth, which Buddhists call the *dharma* or *dhamma*, the seeker must reach beyond words and thoughts to the true essence of things. The spiritual quest is not for the ultimate thought or final belief, but for that which does the thinking and the believing.

The water from the ocean contained in a pot can neither be called an ocean nor non-ocean, but it can be called only part of the ocean. Similarly, a doctrine, though arising from the Absolute Truth, is neither the Truth nor not the Truth.

JAINISM: VIDYANANDI, TATTVARTHASLOKAVARTIKA 116

*Sickness arises from total involvement
in the process of misunderstanding
from beginningless time.
It arises from the passions
that result from unreal mental constructions,
and hence ultimately nothing is perceived
which can be said to be sick.
What is the elimination of this sickness?
It is the elimination of egoism and possessiveness.
What is the elimination of egoism and possessiveness?
It is the freedom from dualism.
What is freedom from dualism?
It is the absence of involvement
with either the external or the internal.
What is absence of involvement
with either external or internal?
It is non-deviation, non-fluctuation,
and non-distraction from equanimity.
What is equanimity?
It is the equality of everything from self to liberation.
Why?*

Because both self and liberation are void.

BUDDHISM: HOLY TEACHING OF VIMALAKIRTI 5

Give up conceptualizing altogether. Have no beliefs or concepts of any kind. You are the ever-free Consciousness. How can any thinking help you in any way?

HINDUISM: ASHTAVAKRA GITA 145

Lord Mahavira said to Gautama, "When Dharma is not seen by the seer directly, it is seen through the wire mesh of words. Conjecture is the wire mesh that covers that window. Multiple sects and systems result from such an indirect observation. The path suggested to you, Gautama, is the direct path of the seer: Be vigilant and a seer of Dharma."

JAINISM: UTTARADHYAYANA SUTRA 10.31

*Of all things seen in the world
Only mind is the host;
By grasping forms according to interpretation
It becomes deluded, not true to reality.*

*All philosophies in the world
Are mental fabrications;
There has never been a single doctrine
By which one could enter the true essence of things.*

*By the power of perceiver and perceived
All kinds of things are born;
They soon pass away, not staying,
Dying out instant to instant.*

BUDDHISM: GARLAND SUTRA 10

A RAFT TO THE FARTHER SHORE

In his famous parable of the raft, the Buddha explains that his teachings are not a destination, but a means of traveling. They are the raw materials from which we can build for ourselves a raft of understanding and, by our own effort, make the spiritual journey. Teachings help us across the sea to the safety of the farther shore, where they become redundant, even an encumbrance. If one should not be attached to wise teachings, the Buddha concludes, how much more should one not be attached to foolishness?

The Taoist sage Chuang Tzu gives us a similar image for the role of ideas. They are traps to catch meaning which, when successful, have served their purpose and become quite useless. Where, he wonders, can he find a man who has gone beyond words? Such a man would truly be worth having a word with!

LEFT
Gilt-copper statue of Gautama the Buddha, Nepalese.

O monks, a man is on a journey. He comes to a vast stretch of water.
On this side the shore is dangerous, but on the other it is safe and without danger.
No boat goes to the other shore nor is there any bridge for crossing over. He says to
himself, "This sea of water is vast, and the shore on this side is full of danger; but on
the other shore it is safe and without danger. No boat goes to the other side, nor is
there a bridge for crossing over. It would be good therefore if I would gather grass,
wood, branches, and leaves to make a raft, and with the help of the raft cross over
safely to the other side, exerting myself with my hands and feet."
Then that man gathers grass, wood, branches, and leaves and makes a raft, and with
the help of that raft crosses over safely to the other side, exerting himself with his
hands and feet. Having crossed over and gotten to the other side, he thinks,
"This raft was of great help to me. With its aid I have crossed safely over to this side.
It would be good if I carry this raft on my head or on my back wherever I go."
What do you think, O monks, if he acted in this way would that man be acting
properly with regard to the raft?
"No, sir."
In which way, then, would he be acting properly with regard to the raft? Having
crossed and gone over to the other side, suppose that man should think,
"This raft was a great help to me. With its aid I have crossed safely over to this side,
exerting myself with my hands and feet. It would be good if I beached this raft on the
shore, or moored it and left it afloat, and then went on my way wherever it may be."
Acting in this way that man would act properly with regard to the raft.
In the same manner, O monks, I have taught a doctrine similar to a raft – it is for
crossing over, and not for carrying. You who understand that the teaching is similar to
a raft, should give up attachment to even the good Dhamma;
how much more then should you give up evil things.

BUDDHISM: MAJJHIMA NIKAYA I. 134–5

The fish trap exists because of the
fish; once you've gotten the fish, you
can forget the trap. The rabbit snare
exists because of the rabbit; once
you've gotten the rabbit, you can
forget the snare. Words exist because
of meaning; once you've gotten the
meaning, you can forget the words.
Where can I find a man who has
forgotten words so I can have a word
with him?

TAOISM: CHUANG TZU 26

GNOSIS

The ancient pagans and early Gnostic Christians called spiritual knowledge *gnosis*. To them, scriptures and doctrines were of little value compared with a direct personal experience through which an individual could know the truth firsthand. In the ancient mystery religions the Higher Self was called a *daemon* and the lower self an *idolon* meaning "image or idol." The lower self is like an illusionary reflection of the Higher Self and experiences gnosis when it recognizes this sublime fact. The author of a gnostic poem attributed to King Solomon conveys something of this mystical experience, exclaiming "I drank and was drunk with the living water that never dies, and my drunkenness gave me knowledge."

In the Gnostic scripture The Book of Thomas the Contender, Jesus addresses his twin Judas Thomas. *Thomas* means "twin." Whether Jesus actually had such a brother is unimportant. To the Gnostics, Jesus the Christ is a symbol of the Higher Self, and Thomas, his disciple and twin, a symbol of the lower self. In the same way that gnosis is imparted to Thomas by his savior, the Gnostics believed that each one of us can receive this spiritual knowledge from the Higher Self within.

These are the secret words that the savior spoke to Judas Thomas which I, Mathaias, wrote down while I was walking, listening to them speak with one another.

The savior said, "Brother Thomas, while you have time in the world, listen to me, and I will reveal to you the things you have pondered in your mind. Now since it has been said that you are my twin and true companion, examine yourself and learn who you are, in what way you exist, and how you will come to be. Since you will be called my brother, it is not fitting that you be ignorant of yourself. And I know that you have understood, because you have already understood that I am the knowledge of the truth.

So while you accompany me, although you are uncomprehending, you have in fact already come to know, and you will be called 'the one who knows himself.' For he who has not known himself has known nothing, but he who has known himself has at the same time already achieved knowledge about the depth of the all. So then, you, my brother Thomas, have beheld what is obscure to men, that is, what they ignorantly stumble against."

THE BOOK OF THOMAS THE CONTENDER

LEFT
Detail, The Tree of Jesse, *Romanian, 16th century.*

My heart was cloven and there
appeared a flower,
and grace Sprang up
and fruit from the Lord,

for the highest one split me
with his holy spirit,
exposed my love for him
and filled me with his love.

His splitting of my heart was
my salvation
and I followed the way of his peace,
the way of truth.

From the beginning to the end
I received his knowledge.

and sat on the rock of truth
where he placed me.

Speaking waters came near my lip
from the vast fountain of the Lord,

and I drank and was drunk
with the living water that never dies,
and my drunkenness gave me
knowledge.

I threw off vanity,
turned to my God
and his bounty made me rich.

I threw off the madness of the earth,
I stripped it from me
and cast it away,

and the Lord renewed me
in his raiment
and held me in his light.

From above he gave me
uncorrupt ease
and I was like land deep and happy
in its orchards,
and the Lord was sun on the
face of the land.

My eyes were clear,
dew was on my face.

and my nostrils enjoyed
the aroma of the Lord.

JUDAISM AND CHRISTIANITY: ODES OF
SOLOMON 11

LIVING KNOWLEDGE

Spiritual knowledge is a living experience, not wise words in old books. "If the Self of which the scriptures speak is not known by the seeker, what use are scriptures to him?" asks the Svetasvatara Upanishad. The Hindu sage Sankara declares that liberation does not come through learning, but only through awakening to oneness. The Gospel of Peace of Jesus Christ advises searching for the living law, not the written word. God is nearer to us than scripture and his law is revealed in nature around us and within ourselves.

He who does not know that indestructible Being of the Rig Veda, that highest ether-like Self wherein all the gods reside, of what use is the Rig Veda to him? Those only who know It rest contented.

HINDUISM: SVETASVATARA UPANISHAD 4.8

Seek not the law in your scriptures, for the law is life, whereas the scripture is dead. I tell you truly, Moses received not his laws from God in writing, but through the living word. The law is living word of living God to living prophets for living men.

In everything that is life is the law written. You find it in the grass, in the tree, in the river, in the mountain, in the birds of heaven, in the fishes of the sea; but seek it chiefly in yourselves. For I tell you truly, all living things are nearer to God than the scripture which is without life.

God so made life and all living things that they might by the everliving word teach the laws of the true God to man. God wrote not the laws in the pages of books, but in your heart and in your spirit. I tell you truly, that the scripture is the work of man, but life and all its hosts are the work of our God.

CHRISTIANITY: THE GOSPEL OF PEACE OF JESUS CHRIST

Not by Yoga nor by works nor by knowledge, but only through awaking to the oneness of one's true Self with the Eternal, does liberation come, and in no other way.

Well uttered speech, a waterfall of words and skill in setting forth the sacred texts and learning are for the delectation of the learned, but do not bring liberation.

Not by weapons, nor scriptures, not by wind nor fire, can this bondage be loosed, nor by myriads of ritual acts, without the great sword of discerning knowledge, sharp and keen, through divine grace.

He who is convinced of the truth of the sacred teaching faithfully performs all duties; by this comes self-purification; when his intelligence is purified, the vision of the supreme Self comes; thereby he destroys birth and death, root and all.

HINDUISM: SANKARA, THE CREST JEWEL OF WISDOM

LEFT
*Illuminated text of
St. Matthew,
Belgian, c. 750.*

KNOWLEDGE WITHOUT OPINIONS

Spiritual knowledge is not a set of clever opinions. Ironically, it is found through a humble acknowledgment of our profound ignorance in the face of the mystery of life. The ancient pagan oracle of Delphi announced that the philosopher Socrates was the wisest man alive, because he knew he knew nothing. This sort of wise ignorance is seen as a virtue in the mystical traditions of all religions. The Sufi master Rumi compares reason to a moth irresistibly drawn to the light of the Beloved (God), where it is consumed in the flames. The nature of reason is to seek for God, but God's nature is to be forever beyond its reach. Yet through the process of searching for intellectual understanding, the mind is drawn into the light where it is consumed, leaving the seeker ignorant *about* God, but at one *with* God.

Human opinions are toys for children.

ANCIENT MYSTERY RELIGIONS: HERACLITUS LVIII

To discover the maker and father of the universe is indeed a hard task, and having found him it would be impossible to tell any one about him.

ANCIENT MYSTERY RELIGIONS: PLATO, TIMAEUS

It is healthy to know you know nothing.
Pretending to know is a kind of sickness.
Realizing you are ill,
is the beginning of healing.
The Wise are sick of sickness,
and so they are well.

TAOISM: TAO TE CHING 71

Knowledge puffs up, but love builds up.
If any one imagines that he knows something,
he does not yet know as he ought to know.
But if one loves God, one is known by him.

CHRISTIANITY: 1 CORINTHIANS 8.1–3

Whoever goes after unreasonable and unnecessary rationalization will never be able to reach truth.

ISLAM: NAHJUL BALAGHA, SAYING 30

Reason is like a moth, and the Beloved is like a candle. When the moth dashes itself against the candle, it is consumed and destroyed. But the moth is so by nature, that however much it may be hurt by that consuming agony, it cannot do without the candle.
If there were any animal like the moth that could not do without the light of the candle and dashed itself against that light, it would itself be a moth; whilst if the moth dashed itself against the light of the candle and the moth were not consumed, that indeed would not be a candle. Therefore the man who can do without God and makes no effort is no man at all; whilst if he were able to comprehend God, that indeed would not be God. Therefore the true man is he who is never free from striving, who revolves restlessly and ceaselessly about the light of the Majesty of God. And God is He who consumes man and makes him naught, being incomprehensible by reason.

ISLAM: DISCOURSE OF RUMI 9

ABOVE
Islamic painting of the holy man and his disciples, Isfahan, mid-17th century.

THE DAZZLING DARKNESS

The Hindu Brihad Aranyaka Upanishad teaches that God can only be known through *neti neti* – not this, not that. What God is can never be said, so we must reveal him by stripping away all that He is not. The Christian mystic St. Dionysius presents a similar idea. We must be like sculptors carving a statue by chipping away all that obscures the beautiful image hidden in the stone. We must dismiss all we think we know – not this, not that – and plunge into the darkness of not knowing. To find true knowledge we must "know behind the mind by knowing nothing." Dionysius asks us to find the light by embracing the darkness, which he calls the Dazzling Darkness of God. This is consciousness itself, unilluminated because it is the light which illuminates all.

BELOW
Buddha.

The good cause of all is both eloquent and taciturn, indeed wordless. It has neither word nor act of understanding, since it is on a plane above all this, and it is made manifest only to those who travel through foul and fair, who pass beyond the summit of every holy ascent, who leave behind them every divine light, every voice, every word from heaven, and who plunge into the darkness where, as scripture proclaims, there dwells the One who is beyond all things.

Moses breaks away from what sees and is seen, and he plunges into the truly mysterious darkness of unknowing. Here, renouncing all that the mind may conceive, wrapped entirely in the intangible and the invisible, he belongs completely to Him who is beyond everything. Here, being neither oneself nor someone else, one is supremely united by a completely unknowing inactivity of all knowledge, and knows beyond the mind by knowing nothing.

I pray we could come to this

darkness so far above light! If only we lacked sight and knowledge so as to see, so as to know, unseeing and unknowing, that which lies beyond all vision and knowledge. For this would be really to see and to know: to praise the Transcendent One in a transcending way, namely through the denial of all beings. We would be like sculptors who set out to carve a statue. They remove every obstacle to the pure view of the hidden image, and simply by this act of clearing aside they show up the beauty which is hidden.

CHRISTIANITY: PSEUDO DIONYSIUS, THE
MYSTICAL THEOLOGY, CH. 2

WISE FOOLISHNESS

A delightfully playful line in the Jewish Midrash is "And Solomon became wiser than all men – even than idiots." The wise can seem foolish, and the seemingly foolish may in fact be wise. A Taoist story teaches the mystical paradox of wise foolishness. Master Lieh Tzu and his disciples go to visit another master called Nan-kuo Tzu. He appears very withdrawn and is frightful to look at. Nan-kuo Tzu ignores Lieh Tzu completely, but spontaneously talks pleasantly to some of the disciples at the back of the gathering. Lieh Tzu's followers are confused by Nan-kuo Tzu's bizarre behavior, so Lieh Tzu explains:

BELOW
The visit of a Rajput chief to a hermit residing in a leaf-built hut, Indian, c. 1756.

The disciples were astonished at this, and when they got home again, all wore a puzzled expression. Their master Lieh Tzu said to them: "He who has reached the highest stage of thought is silent. He who has attained to perfect knowledge says nothing. He who uses silence in lieu of speech really does speak. He who for knowledge substitutes blankness of mind really does know. Without words and speaking not, without knowledge and knowing not, he really speaks and really knows. Saying nothing and knowing nothing, there is in reality nothing that he does not say, nothing that he does not know. This is how the matter stands, and there is nothing further to be said. Why are you so astonished without cause?"

TAOISM: LIEH TZU

CHAPTER FIVE

The Good Life

ALL RELIGIONS TEACH that we should live a good life. For Jews, Christians, and Muslims, this means obeying God's commandments. For Buddhists, it means following the Dharma or Laws of Life. For Taoists it means following the Tao or Natural Way – choosing a way of life that reflects the way life is. From a spiritual perspective, however, all of these traditions are saying essentially the same thing. Each one of us is a part of the greater whole, and to live a good life, we must play our part in perfect harmony with the whole.

Scriptures prescribe different moral laws to help us to live a good life. Underlying all of them, however, are a few simple universal themes: Treat others in the same way that we would wish to be treated. Avoid being judgmental as this divides us from others. Repent of our own failings, but accept and forgive the failings of others, just as God accepts and forgives us. These moral laws can be seen as the spiritual counterparts of the physical laws of nature. Just as understanding the laws of nature is a prerequisite for living in harmony with the natural world, so understanding moral laws is a prerequisite for living in harmony with God and with each other.

Madame Helena P. Blavatsky, the founder of the Theosophical Society, points out that, from a spiritual point of view, there is essentially only one moral problem. In *The Key to Theosophy* she writes, "We say that 'Good' and 'Harmony,' and 'Evil' and 'Disharmony' are synonymous. Further we maintain that illness, pain and suffering are results of want of Harmony, and that the one terrible and only cause to the disturbance of Harmony is selfishness in some form or another." At the heart of all moral codes is the development of selflessness. This is more than a noble sentiment. It is a spiritual practice which can release us from the prison of the separate self and lead us to knowledge of the Oneness of God.

Truly understanding the spirit of selflessness expressed in the moral codes of scripture allows us to move beyond blind obedience to an external authority. Rather, we act in ways that express the natural goodness of the Higher Self. Rules and regulations are no longer needed because we spontaneously act well. The moral law is not designed to enslave us, but to set us free to be our Self.

OPPOSITE
*Moses on Mount
Sinai from the
Lambeth Bible,
c. 1140–1150.*

GOD'S LAW

God is often pictured as a lawmaker whose divine decrees are contained within sacred scripture. Various traditions offer different versions of the moral laws by which we should live, but essentially all of them urge us to develop the same good qualities. These bring us closer to God, who is all goodness. Indeed, our word *God* is derived from a Germanic source meaning "The Good."

Breaking God's laws is often described as "evil." This is a strong word that has come to convey the complete opposite of God's goodness. It leads us to picture a great divide, with God on one side and evil on the other. This dichotomy is a misunderstanding, however. The word *evil* is from a Germanic root which originally conveyed "exceeding proper limits." In their original languages the terms used by the scriptures do not convey a sense of permanent alienation from God, but rather a condition of temporary inadequacy. Jesus used the Aramaic term *bisha* which means "unripe" or "inappropriate." The Greek New Testament word usually translated as *sin* means "missing the mark." When we break God's moral law, it a sign that we are "unripe." We are not evil in the modern sense. We are just not yet spiritually mature. Out of ignorance, we are acting contrary to our real essential nature.

Not killing, no longer stealing, forsaking the wives of others, refraining completely from false, divisive, harsh and senseless speech, forsaking covetousness, harmful intent, and the views of Nihilists – these are the ten white paths of action, their opposites are black.

BUDDHISM: NAGARJUNA, PRECIOUS GARLAND 8–9

Forgiveness, humility, straightforwardness, purity, truthfulness, self-restraint, austerity, renunciation, nonattachment, and chastity with one's spouse. These are the ten duties of lay people.

JAINISM: TATTVARTHASUTRA 9.6, P. 112

Nonviolence, truthfulness, not stealing, purity, control of the senses – this, in brief, says Manu, is the Dharma for all the four castes.

HINDUISM: LAWS OF MANU 10.63

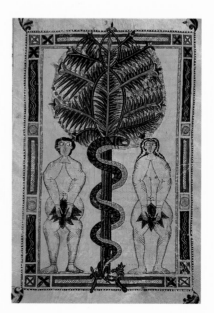

LEFT
Adam and Eve – original sin, Spanish, 10th century.

You shall have no other gods before me.

You shall not make for yourself a graven image in the likeness of anything that is in heaven above, or that is on the earth beneath, or that is in the water; you shall not bow down to them or serve them; for I am a jealous God, visiting the iniquity of the fathers upon the children to the third and fourth generation of those who turn from me, but showing steadfast love to thousands of those who love me and keep my commandments.

You shall not take the name of the Lord your God in vain: for the Lord will not hold him guiltless who takes his name in vain.

Remember to keep the Sabbath day holy. Six days you shall labor, and do all your work; but the seventh day is a Sabbath to the Lord your God; in it you shall not do any work, you, or your son, or your daughter, your manservant, or your maidservant, or your cattle, or the sojourner who is within your gates; for in six days the Lord made heaven and earth, the sea, and all that is in them, and rested on the seventh day; therefore the Lord blessed the Sabbath day and hallowed it.

Honor your father and your mother, that your days may be long in the land which the Lord your God gives you.

You shall not kill.

You shall not commit adultery.

You shall not steal.

You shall not bear false witness against your neighbor.

You shall not covet your neighbor's house; you shall not covet your neighbor's wife, or his manservant, or his maidservant, or his ox, or his ass, or anything that is your neighbor's.

JUDAISM AND CHRISTIANITY: EXODUS 20.1–17

BELOW
Fresco showing Adam and Eve with the tree and serpent, Norwegian, 1200.

Say, Come, I will recite what God has made a sacred duty for you: Ascribe nothing as equal with Him. Be good to your parents. Kill not your children on a plea of want. We provide sustenance for you and for them. Approach not lewd behavior whether open or in secret. Take not life, which God has made sacred, except by way of justice and law. This He commands you, that you may learn wisdom. And approach not the property of the orphan, except to improve it, until he attains the age of maturity.

Give full measure and weight, in justice. No burden do We place on any soul but that which it can bear. And if you give your word, do it justice, even if a near relative is concerned; and fulfill your obligations before God. This He commands you, that you may remember. This is My straight Path: follow it, and do not follow other paths which will separate you from My Path. This He commands you, that you may be righteous.

ISLAM: QUR'AN 6.151–3

[69]

HARMONY WITH NATURE

The Stoic philosopher Epictetus (*c*.55–135 C.E.) was born a slave and lived to become the spiritual master of the Roman emperor Marcus Aurelius Antoninus, who himself also became a great Stoic philosopher. Epictetus teaches that a happy life and a virtuous life are the same thing. Such a life is equally available to all, regardless of wealth or social position. He emphasizes moral progress rather than achieving moral perfection. He does not teach rules to follow, but advises us to live in harmony with the laws of nature.

For Epictetus, suffering is not caused by what life brings us, but by how we choose to view things. We can not change what happens to us, but we can change our harmful opinions and attitudes. His teachings are reminiscent of Taoist scriptures that advise us that to live in harmony with the flow of the Tao, we need only to let things be as they are.

Don't try to make your own rules.

Conduct yourself in all matters, grand and public or small and domestic, in accordance with the laws of nature. Harmonizing your will with nature should be your utmost ideal.

Where do you practice this ideal? In the particulars of your own daily life with its uniquely personal tasks and duties. When you carry out your tasks, such as taking a bath, do so, to the best of your ability, in harmony with nature. When you eat, do so, to the best of your ability, in harmony with nature, and so on.

It is not so much what you are doing as how you are doing it. When we properly understand and live by this principle, while difficulties will arise – for they are part of the divine order too – inner peace will still be possible. Things themselves don't hurt or hinder us. Nor do other people. How we view these things is another matter. It is our attitudes and

reactions that give us trouble. Therefore, even death is no big deal in and of itself. It is our notion of death, our idea that it is terrible, that terrifies us. There are so many different ways to think about death. Scrutinize your notions about death – and everything else. Are they really true? Are they doing you any good? Don't dread death or pain; dread the fear of death or pain.

ANCIENT MYSTERY RELIGIONS: EPICTETUS

LEFT
The Celtic Underworld, Erinn.

INNER VIGILANCE

The Hindu Allama Prabhu and Buddhist Dhammapada teach that to live a good life, we have to master our own self. The moral dilemmas that we face are not "out there" in the world. They are caused by our own selfish cravings. Nothing is intrinsically an evil temptation. It is only our reactions that make something morally dangerous.

They say that woman
is an enticement.
No, No, she is not so.
They say that money
is an enticement.
No, No, it is not so.
They say that landed property
is an enticement.
No, No, it is not so.
The real enticement is the insatiable
appetite of the mind,
O Lord Guheswara!

HINDUISM: ALLAMA PRABHU, VACANA 91

Your worst enemy cannot harm you
as much as your own thoughts
unguarded.

But once mastered,
no one can help you as much,
not even your father or your mother.

BUDDHISM: DHAMMAPADA 3

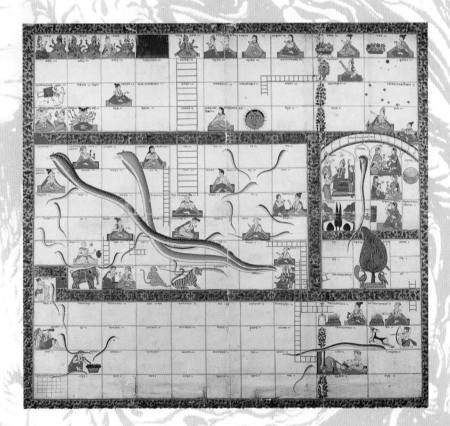

LEFT
Snakes and ladders –
the path to heaven
or hell, mid-18th
century.

THE PRICE OF VICE

Scripture teaches that when we act badly we do not just harm others, but also ourselves. If we sin, we have to live with the knowledge of our actions. If we are angry with another, we experience the destructive rage as well. With every selfish act or thought we become entrapped in our separateness, which instantly impoverishes our lives. With every selfless act, however, we free ourselves from our separateness, and our lives are instantly richer.

Wabisah ibn Ma'bad said, "I went to see the Messenger of God and he said to me, 'You want to question me on the subject of virtue?' 'Yes,' I replied, and he went on, 'Question your heart. Virtue is that by which the soul enjoys repose and the heart tranquility. Sin is what introduces trouble into the soul and tumult into man's bosom – and this despite the religious advice which men may give you.'"

ISLAM: FORTY HADITH OF AN-NAWAWI 27

*Why, sir, do you get angry
at someone
Who is angry with you?
What are you going to gain by it?
How is he going to lose by it?
Your physical anger brings
dishonor on yourself;
Your mental anger
disturbs your thinking.
How can the fire in your house burn
the neighbor's house
Without engulfing your own?*

HINDUISM: BASAVANNA, VACANA 248

A man who has committed one of the deadly sins will never again, until his death, lose the thought of that action; he cannot get rid of it or remove it, but it follows after him until the time of his death.

BUDDHISM: PERFECTION OF WISDOM IN
EIGHT THOUSAND LINES 17.3

*Ashes fly back in the face of him
who throws them.*

AFRICAN WISDOM PROVERB: YORUBA,
NIGERIA

LEFT
*Late 13th-century
illumination by
Maître Honoré,
showing Mercy and
Avarice, Lot and the
Angels, and the
Prudent Woman
with her oil.*

THE FIRST SHALL BE LAST

Scripture teaches that if we put ourselves first, God will put us last. If we put ourselves last, we shall be put first. If we aggrandize ourselves, life will humble us. If we humble ourselves, life will elevate us. If we serve the separate self, we will end up impoverished and confined. If we are selfless, we will be liberated into our true divine nature.

ABOVE
Mosaic showing the widow's mite, Italian, 6th century.

Give up, and you will succeed.
Bow and you will stand tall.
Be empty and you will be filled.
Let go of the old, and let in the new.
Have little, and there is room
to receive more.
The wise stand out,
because they see themselves
as part of the Whole.
They shine,
because they don't want to impress.
They achieve great things,
because they don't look
for recognition.
Their wisdom is contained
in what they are,
not their opinions.
They refuse to argue,
so no one argues with them.
The Ancients said:
"Give up and you will succeed."
Is this empty nonsense?
Try it.
If you are sincere,
you will find fulfillment.

TAOISM: TAO TE CHING 22

Him who humbles himself God exalts; him who exalts himself God humbles; from him who searches for greatness, greatness flies; him who flies from greatness, greatness searches out: with him who is importunate with circumstance, circumstance is importunate; by him who gives way to circumstance, circumstance stands.

JUDAISM: TALMUD, ERUBIN 13B

Blessed are the poor in spirit, for theirs is the kingdom of heaven.
Blessed are those who mourn, for they shall be comforted.
Blessed are the meek, for they shall inherit the earth.
Blessed are those who hunger and thirst for righteousness, for they shall be satisfied.
Blessed are the merciful, for they shall obtain mercy.
Blessed are the pure in heart, for they shall see God.
Blessed are the peacemakers, for they shall be called sons of God.
Blessed are those who are persecuted for righteousness' sake, for theirs is the kingdom of heaven.

CHRISTIANITY: MATTHEW 5.3–10

The last will be first, and the first last. Whoever exalts himself will be humbled, and whoever humbles himself will be exalted.

CHRISTIANITY: MATTHEW 20.16 AND 23.12

Outwardly, we are last of all, but inwardly we preceded everyone.

ISLAM: HADITH OF BUKHARI

ABOVE
Siddhartha, the future Buddha, and his groom, mounted on horses, Chinese, 10th century.

REPENTANCE

All religions urge us to repent of our shortcomings, as a first and important step on the road to transforming them. In the ancient mystery religions, initiates into the mysteries were required to make public confessions of their sins. Some Taoist schools have made use of the same technique, as does Catholicism in a more personal way in the confessional. As it says in the Buddhist Mahaparinirvana Sutra, "If one hides the evil, it adds and grows. If one bares it and repents, the sin dies out."

Repentance is a means of purification. When unacknowledged, the inner knowledge that we have acted badly grows into the cancer of guilt. Once acknowledged, it can be transformed by the healing power of repentance into wisdom; leaving us free to leave the past behind and live again. Repentance is not about seeing how bad we are. It clears away the accumulated debris of the past and reveals our natural goodness.

*Let every person ask pardon of the
Great Light Asis,
The Molder of us all.*

INDIGENOUS RELIGIONS: KIPSIGIS SAYING
FROM KENYA

If one has, indeed, done deeds of wickedness, but afterward alters his way and repents, resolved not to do anything wicked, but to practice reverently all that is good, he is sure in the long run to obtain good fortune – this is called changing calamity into blessing.

TAOISM: TREATISE ON RESPONSE AND
RETRIBUTION 5

*By public confession, repentance, penance, repetition of holy mantras, and by gifts, the sinner is released from guilt.
In proportion as a man who has done wrong, himself confesses it, even so is he freed from guilt, as a snake from its slough.
In proportion as his heart loathes his evil deed, even so far is his body freed from that guilt.*

HINDUISM: LAWS OF MANU 11.228–30

LEFT
The Prodigal Son,
*Palma il Vecchio
(1480-1528).*

If one hides the evil, it adds and grows. If one bares it and repents, the sin dies out. Therefore all Buddhas say that the wise do not hide sin.

BUDDHISM: MAHAPARINIRVANA SUTRA 560

Sin disappears with repentance. Does not darkness vanish simultaneously with exposure to light? Those who do not repent, retain their sins. Is it not true that unexposed darkness remains darkness? Confession may be made in secret, or you may write a letter to a leader of the teachings. However, there is nothing to be gained by disclosing your sin in darkness or before people who will only ridicule you. What is the use of exposing darkness to darkness? When once man sincerely repents, from that very instant his original perfection as a child of God becomes manifested as if his whole being were cleansed and purified. After sincerely repenting, you feel at peace within yourself because you are truly My children and I am one with all of you. Divine Spirit flows abundantly through you, and your spirit will grow and finally attain Infinite Life.

SHINTO: SEICHO-NO-IE, HOLY SUTRA FOR SPIRITUAL HEALING

A Pharisee and a tax collector went to the temple to pray. The Pharisee stood tall and prayed "I thank you God, that I am different to other men – extortioners, adulterers, or the likes of that tax collector. I fast twice a week and give tithes of all that I get." The tax collector, on the other hand, beat his breast without even lifting his eyes to heaven, praying "Be merciful God, I am a sinner!" I tell you, this man returned home justified in God's sight, not the other; for every one who exalts himself will be humbled, but he who humbles himself will be exalted.

CHRISTIANITY: LUKE 18.10-14

There was a rich chief tax collector named Zacchaeus, who stood and said to the Lord, "Look Lord, I give half of my goods to the poor, and if I have defrauded anyone of anything, I pay it back four times over." And Jesus said to him, "Today salvation has come to this house."

CHRISTIANITY: LUKE 19.2,8–9

The sin which makes you sad and repentant is liked better by the Lord than the good deed which turns you vain and conceited.

ISLAM: NAHJUL BALAGHA, SAYING 44

DO NOT BE JUDGMENTAL

Scripture teaches us to look to our own failings, but only to see the best in others. We cannot know the individual predicaments that others face in their lives and are in no position to judge anyone. When we are judgmental we distance ourselves from others and trap ourselves in our own separateness. When we see the best in others, we reach out across the divide that separates us.

Do not judge another until you have walked some miles in his moccasins.

INDIGENOUS RELIGIONS: NATIVE AMERICAN SAYING

Do not judge your comrade until you have stood in his place.

JUDAISM: ABOT 2.5

Early in the morning Jesus went to the temple once more and many people came to see him. While he was sitting giving teachings, some scribes and Pharisees brought a woman who had been caught in adultery and placed her in the middle of the group of people. They asked, "Teacher, this woman has been caught in the act of adultery. In the Law, Moses decreed that we should stone such a woman to death. What do you say?" They said this to catch him out, so that they might have some offence to charge him with. Jesus bent down and wrote with his finger in the dust. But as they persisted to demand an answer, he stood up and said to them, "Let the one among you who has never sinned throw the first stone at her." And then he bent down again and continued writing with his finger in the dust. When they heard this, they went away, one by one, beginning with the eldest, and Jesus was left alone with the woman standing before him. Jesus looked up and said to her, "Woman, where is everyone? Has no one condemned you?" She said, "No one, Master." And Jesus said, "Neither do I condemn you. Go on your way and do not sin again."

CHRISTIANITY: JOHN 8.2–11

LEFT
Young Christ teaching in the temple, early 14th century.

Don't judge others and you will not be judged. For you will be judged by the the judgments that you pronounce. What you give will be what you get. Why do you see the speck of sawdust in your brother's eye, but don't notice the log in your own eye? How can you say to your brother, "Let me take the speck out of your eye," when there is a log in your own eye? You hypocrite. First take the log out of your own eye. Then you will see clearly enough to remove the speck from your brother's eye.

CHRISTIANITY: MATTHEW 7.1–5 P.703

Confucius said, "Attack the evil that is within yourself; do not attack the evil that is in others."

CONFUCIANISM: ANALECTS 12.21

The vile are ever prone to detect the faults of others, though they be as small as mustard seeds, and persistently shut their eyes against their own, though they be as large as Vilva fruit.

HINDUISM: GARUDA PURANA 112

*Dwelling on your brother's faults multiplies your own.
You are far from the end of your journey.*

BUDDHISM: DHAMMAPADA 18

We cannot choose our external circumstances, but we can always choose how we respond to them. If it is our feelings about things that torment us rather than the things themselves, it follows that blaming others is silly. Therefore, when we suffer setbacks, disturbances, or grief, let us never place the blame on others, but on our own attitudes. Small-minded people habitually reproach others for their own misfortunes. Average people reproach themselves. Those who are dedicated to a life of wisdom understand that the impulse to blame something or someone is foolishness, that there is nothing to be gained in blaming, whether it be others or oneself. One of the signs of the dawning of moral progress is the gradual extinguishing of blame. We see the futility of finger-pointing. The more we examine our attitudes and work on ourselves, the less we are apt to be swept away by stormy emotional reactions in which we seek easy explanations for unbidden events. Things simply are what they are. Other people think what they will think; it is of no concern to us. No Shame. No Blame.

ANCIENT MYSTERY RELIGIONS: EPICTETUS

FORGIVENESS

ABOVE
*Christ taking on the
sins of the world.*

Scripture teaches that we should forgive those who wrong us. Through an awareness of our own shortcomings we develop the capacity to accept the shortcomings of others. Towards the end of his life, Mahatma Gandhi was asked how he could be so tolerant of people who oppressed him. He answered that when one is truly aware of one's own failings it is easier to deal more compassionately with all the other "rogues." Forgiveness unites us with those from whom we have been divided. As a Jewish Talmudic saying puts it, "Who is the bravest hero? He who turns his enemy into a friend" (Nathan, 23).

Christianity is a religion of forgiveness. It teaches that by following the example of Jesus we are forgiven by God and that we should in like manner forgive others. Jesus counsels us to love our enemies. This is a truly remarkable request. He is not asking us to like our enemies or to approve of what they do, but to love them, to sense an essential unity that we share even with those from whom we feel most alienated. Such love allows us to see those who act with cruelty and malice not as intrinsically bad and therefore unlovable, but as tragically trapped in their selfishness and suffering through this separation from God.

"Two wrongs do not make a right," the old maxim goes. The scriptures teach that if we meet evil with evil then nothing changes. If we meet evil with goodness, then the situation may miraculously be transformed. The evil man is a prisoner of his self. Retaliating against him with anger securely locks the prison doors. Responding with kindness and compassion allows him the opportunity to step free.

The Talmud reminds us of our essential unity and compares seeking vengeance to cutting one's hand while handling a knife and then revenging this violence by stabbing the other hand. When we know we are all one, vengeance is ridiculous and forgiveness is natural.

ABOVE
*Miniature showing
the story of Jacob,
Turkish, 1595.*

A superior being does not render evil for evil; this is a maxim one should observe; the ornament of virtuous persons is their conduct. One should never harm the wicked or the good or even criminals meriting death. A noble soul will ever exercise compassion even toward those who enjoy injuring others or those of cruel deeds when they are actually committing them – for who is without fault?

HINDUISM: RAMAYANA, YUDDHA KANDA 115

Those who beat you with fists, Do not pay them in the same coin, But go to their house and kiss their feet.

SIKHISM: ADI GRANTH, SHALOK, FARID

Where there is forgiveness, there is God Himself.

SIKHISM: ADI GRANTH, SHALOK, KABIR

The best deed of a great man is to forgive and forget.

ISLAM: NAHJUL BALAGHA, SAYING 201

After an attempt at reconciliation, if bitterness still remains – what then? Meet bitterness with kindness.

The Wise act well
without demanding others do.
Someone who ignores
Natural Goodness,
is always concerned that they are
properly honored.
Someone who knows
Natural Goodness
honors their side of the relationship,
regardless.

TAOISM: TAO TE CHING 79

Moses son of Imran said, "My Lord, who is the greatest of Your servants in Your estimation?" and received the reply, "The one who forgives when he is in a position of power."

ISLAM: HADITH OF BAIHAQI

The good deed and the evil deed are not alike. Repel the evil deed with one which is better, then someone with whom you were divided by enmity will become like a bosom friend.

ISLAM: QUR'AN 4.34–35

Who takes vengeance or bears a grudge acts like one who, having cut one hand while handling a knife, avenges himself by stabbing the other hand.

JUDAISM: JERUSALEM TALMUD, NEDARIM 9.4

Peter asked Jesus, "Master, how many times should I forgive my brother if he continues to wrong me? Is seven times enough?" Jesus said to him, "No. Not seven times, but seventy times seven!"

CHRISTIANITY: MATTHEW 18.21-35

Subvert anger by forgiveness.

JAINISM: SAMANASUTTAM 136

You have heard the saying "An eye for an eye and a tooth for a tooth." But I say to you, don't resist evil with evil. If someone strikes you on your right cheek, turn the other one to him as well; and if someone wants to sue you for your coat, let him also have your cloak; and if someone forces you to walk a mile with him, walk with him for two miles; and don't ignore someone who wants to borrow from you, but if you are asked for something, then give it away. You have heard the saying "You shall love your neighbor and hate your enemy." But I say to you, love your enemies and pray for those who persecute you, so that you may be sons of your Heavenly Father. For He makes the sun rise on evil men as well as good men; and sends the rains to unjust men as well as just men. If you love those who love you, is that really a credit to you? Even tax collectors do that! If you honor only your brothers, you are just doing what everyone does, including the foreigners who oppress you! So, you should be perfect like your Heavenly Father.

CHRISTIANITY: MATTHEW 5.38–48

LOVE OTHERS AS YOUR SELF

At the heart of the many ways that scripture advises us to relate to each other lies a universal ethic of empathy. We should treat others as we would wish to be treated, for they are conscious feeling beings who suffer pain and enjoy delights, just as we do. Jains expand this sentiment to include animals, as do Buddhists who pray for the benefit of "all sentient beings."

We disregard the interests of others when we cannot see beyond our own self-interest. Jain scripture reminds us, however, that our deepest self is God. We are all one. We should, therefore, do more than just love others as much as we love ourselves. We should love them as *our own Self.* Our selfishness cuts us off from this experience of unity. Empathizing with others is more than just a way of becoming a better person. It is a profound spiritual practice that leads to an experience of oneness.

What is hateful to you, do not do to your neighbor: that is the whole Torah; all the rest of it is commentary; go and learn.

JUDAISM: TALMUD, SHABBAT 31 A

You shall love your neighbor as yourself.

JUDAISM AND CHRISTIANITY: LEVITICUS 19.18

Treat others as you would wish to be treated.

CHRISTIANITY: MATTHEW 7.12

Do nothing from selfishness or conceit, but in humility count others better than yourselves.

CHRISTIANITY: PHILIPPIANS 2.3

Not one of you is a believer until he loves for his brother what he loves for himself.

ISLAM: FORTY HADITH OF AN-NAWAWI 13

Jesus was asked, "Teacher, which is the greatest commandment in the Law?" He replied, "You shall love God with all your heart, and with all your soul, and with all your mind. This is the greatest and first commandment. And the second is like it, You shall love your neighbor as yourself. All the Law and the teachings of the prophets rest on these two commandments."

CHRISTIANITY: MATTHEW 22.36-40

Try your best to treat others as you would wish to be treated yourself, and you will find that this is the shortest way to goodness.

CONFUCIANISM: MENCIUS VII.A.4

Tsekung asked, "Is there one word that can serve as a principle of conduct for life?" Confucius replied, "The word 'shu' – reciprocity: Do not do to others what you do not want them to do to you."

CONFUCIANISM: ANALECTS 15.23 P.114

ABOVE
Adoration of the Magi, French, c. 1470.

The body is impure, bad-smelling, and replete with various kinds of stench which trickle here and there. If one, possessed of such a body, thinks highly of himself and despises others that is due to nothing other than his lack of insight. Comparing oneself to others in such terms as "Just as I am so are they, just as they are so am I," one should neither kill nor cause others to kill.

BUDDHISM: SUTTA NIPATA 205-6 AND 705

One going to take a pointed stick to pinch a baby bird should first try it on himself to feel how it hurts.

INDIGENOUS RELIGIONS: YORUBA PROVERB
FROM NIGERIA

A man should wander about treating all creatures as he himself would like to be treated.

JAINISM: SUTRAKRITANGA 1.11.33

One should not behave towards others in a way which is disagreeable to oneself. This is the essence of morality. All other activities are due to selfish desire.

HINDUISM: MAHABHARATA, ANUSASANA
PARVA 113.8

One who you think should be hit is none else but you. One who you think should be governed is none else but you. One who you think should be tortured is none else but you. One who you think should be enslaved is none else but you. One who you think should be killed is none else but you. A sage is ingenuous and leads his life after comprehending the parity of the killed and the killer. Therefore, neither does he cause violence to others nor does he make others do so.

JAINISM: ACARANGASUTRA 5.101-2

CONFUCIANISM AND THE NATURAL HEART

Confucianism is often associated with the strict observances of religious rituals and social morality. Here, however, the sage Mencius emphasizes the naturalness of a loving heart. Compassion is an intrinsic human quality, the basis of which is our capacity to empathize with the sufferings of others. Our commitment to the common good arises not from rules and regulations, but from an intrinsic repulsion towards vice. In fact, all of the great qualities valued by Confucianism find their foundation in natural human sentiments, which need only to be fostered and brought out.

Mencius said, "All men have this heart that, when they see another man suffer, they suffer, too. What do I mean? Well, take an example. A man sees a child about to fall into a well. No matter who the man is, his heart will flip-flop, and he will feel the child's predicament; and not because he expects to get something out of it from the child's parents, or because he wants praise from his neighbors, associates, or friends, or because he is afraid of a bad name, or anything like that.

"From this we can see that it is not human not to have a heart that sympathizes with pain. Likewise, not to have a heart that is repelled by vice: that is not human, either. Not to have a heart that is willing to defer: that's not human. And not to have a heart that discriminates between true and false is not human, either.

"What is the foundation of natural human feeling for others? The heart that sympathizes with pain. What is the foundation of a commitment to the common good? The heart that is repelled by vice. What is the foundation of respect for social and religious forms? The heart that is willing to defer. And what is the foundation for a liberal education? The heart that can tell true from false.

"People have these four foundations like they have four limbs. Everybody has these four foundations in them. If these four foundations are fulfilled, it will be like a fire starting up or a spring bursting through. If they are fulfilled, it will be enough to create and preserve order in the world. Leave them unfulfilled, and it will even be impossible for someone to take care of his father and mother."

CONFUCIANISM: MENCIUS II.A.6

ABOVE
*The Rabbi
celebrates Passover,
Jewish prayer book,
14th century.*

LIBERATION FROM THE LAW

Moral laws help us walk the spiritual path, the aim of which is to awaken the natural goodness of the soul. We then require no rules and regulations because we spontaneously act well. If we scrupulously follow the letter of the law yet do not understand it, we will only seem to be good. Our inner spirit will not be set free, but will be confined within external rules and regulations. Lao Tzu advises us to abandon such an attitude and trust our innate nature. Hindu scripture teaches that if we truly awaken to our Higher Self, we are free to do as we please.

St. Paul sees Christ as coming to free us from the law, through faith. The word *faith* has come to mean a sort of blind belief, but this is not what St. Paul means. For him, faith is an intuitive knowledge of God. This frees the spiritual seeker from any external authority, even the scriptural law, because it gives a direct personal insight into the source of the law. St. Paul teaches that the law was only our custodian until Christ made available the knowledge of God.

The word *conscience* means "with knowledge." Our conscience is the part of us that naturally knows how to act well. If we live with knowledge we can simply follow our inner promptings. The Gospel of John tells us that one who is born of spirit acts as spontaneously and naturally as the wind. In the Gnostic Gospel of Thomas, Jesus advises his disciples not to tell lies and not to do what they hate – to simply be honest with others and themselves. If we are true to our innate goodness, we can not do other than act well and will hate acting badly. If we truly know that all is one, how can we wish to harm anyone? The best way of following the moral law is to simply be your Self.

Holding to the letter of the law,
may be appropriate to keep a country
in order.
But only acting from your true being,
is always appropriate.

TAOISM: TAO TE CHING 57

The Master said, "Is Goodness
indeed so far away? If we really
wanted Goodness, we should find
that it was at our very side."

CONFUCIANISM:

ANALECTS 7.29

"Give up trying to seem holy, forget
trying to appear wise, and it will be a
lot better for everyone."
"Abandon trying to seem good,
throw out self righteousness, and
rediscover natural compassion."
"Stop trying to be so smart, quit
being calculating, and you won't
become a rogue."
These three sayings are important,
but I want to add this... Be simple
and true to your own nature.
Be selfless and at peace with the way
things are.

TAOISM: TAO TE CHING 19

When the "me" is present, it is bondage; when the "me" is not present, it is liberation. Having understood this, it should be easy for you to refrain from accepting or rejecting anything.

Absence of attachment to sense-objects is liberation; passion for sense-objects is bondage. Understand this fact, and then do as you please.

HINDUISM: ASHTAVAKRA GITA 127

I have declared to you the Truth, the deepest of all secrets; meditate on it, and then do as you please.

HINDUISM: BHAGAVAD GITA

The wind blows where it wills, and you hear the sound of it, but you do not know where it comes from or where it is going. It is the same with every one who is born of Spirit.

CHRISTIANITY: JOHN 3.8

His disciples questioned him and said to him, "Do you want us to fast? How shall we pray? Shall we give alms? What diet shall we observe?" Jesus said "Do not tell lies and do not do what you hate."

CHRISTIANITY: GNOSTIC GOSPEL OF THOMAS 6

Everyone involved in keeping the demands of the Law is under a curse, for it is written, "Cursed be every one who does not abide by all things written in the Book of the Law, and do them." It is obvious, therefore, that no one is justified before God by the Law. Christ redeemed us from the curse of the Law.

Before faith came, we were confined under the Law, kept under restraint until faith should be revealed. The Law was our custodian until Christ came, that we might be justified by faith. But now that faith has come, we are no longer under a custodian; for through Jesus we are all sons of God, through faith.

CHRISTIANITY: GALATIANS 3.10–13 AND 3.21–26

BELOW
Stone relief of Christ and the pilgrims from Emmaus by Santo Domingo de Silos, Spanish, 12th century.

The spirit not the letter

The Qur'an says, "This He commands you, that you may learn wisdom." Moral laws exist to awaken our own innate understanding of how to live well. This awakening happens only when the spiritual essence is understood. If we scrupulously obey laws, even when doing so is ridiculous, we have completely missed the point. They have not taught us wisdom, but imprisoned us within a rigid framework of rules and regulations which we do not understand.

It so happened that on the Sabbath Jesus was walking through some cornfields. His followers were hungry and began picking the ears of wheat and eating them. The Pharisees saw them and said to Jesus, "Look, your followers are doing something that the Law forbids us to do on the Sabbath." Jesus replied, "Haven't you read what David did when he and his companions were hungry? How he went into the house of God and ate the presentation loaves which are meant to be reserved only for the priests? Haven't you read in the Law that every Sabbath priests can work and yet remain blameless? I'm telling you there is something more important than the temple. You would not have been so quick to condemn the innocent if you had understood the meaning of the scripture, 'I desire compassion and not sacrifice; for the Son of Man is even master of the Sabbath.'"
Leaving there, Jesus went into their synagogue where there happened to be a man with a withered hand. Because they were looking for some heresy to accuse him of, the Pharisees asked Jesus, "Is it lawful to heal on the Sabbath?" Jesus said to them, "Would any of you not rescue one of your sheep which had fallen into a pit on the Sabbath? Well, a man is more valuable than a sheep! It is lawful to do good on the Sabbath." Then he said to the man, "Stretch out your hand." The man stretched it out and it became as healthy as his other hand.

CHRISTIANITY: MATTHEW 12.1–14

The written code kills, but the Spirit gives life.

CHRISTIANITY: 2 CORINTHIANS 3.6 P.574

Ch'un-yu K'un said, "Is it prescribed by the rites that, in giving and receiving, man and woman should not touch each other?"
"It is," said Mencius.
"If one's sister-in-law is drowning, should one stretch out a hand to help her?"
"You'd be a brute not to help your sister-in-law who is drowning. It is prescribed by the rites that, in giving and receiving, man and woman do not touch each other, but in stretching out a helping hand to a drowning sister-in-law one uses one's discretion."

CONFUCIANISM: MENCIUS IV.A. 17

PERFECT LIBERTY

Perfect Liberty Kyodan and Tenrikyo are modern Japanese religions that have developed from Shinto. Perfect Liberty Kyodan sees God as a creative artist who wishes us to live creative lives. If we follow the precepts we can be at perfect liberty and practice at once whatever our first inspiration dictates. Tenrikyo recommends deeds of love and charity to remove the dust which has accumulated over our essential goodness. When the dust is swept away, God will be happy and so will all human beings – a charming statement of the purpose of morality, which is expressed in one way or another by the scriptures of all religions.

1. *Life is art.*
2. *The whole life of the individual is a continuous succession of Self-expression.*
3. *The individual is a manifestation of God.*
4. *We suffer if we do not manifest ourselves.*
5. *We lose our Self if we are swayed by our feelings.*
6. *Our true Self is revealed when our ego is effaced.*
7. *All things exist in mutual relation to one another.*
8. *Live radiantly as the Sun.*
9. *All men are equal.*
10. *Bring mutual happiness through our expressions.*
11. *Depend on God at all times.*
12. *There is always a way for each person.*
13. *There is one way for men, and there is another for women.*
14. *All things exist for world peace.*
15. *Our whole environment is the mirror of our mind.*
16. *All things make progress and develop.*
17. *Grasp the heart of everything.*
18. *At every moment man stands at the crossroad of good and evil.*
19. *Practise at once whatever your first inspiration dictates.*
20. *Attain the perfect harmonious state of mind and matter.*
21. *Live in Perfect Liberty.*

SHINTO: PREFECT LIBERTY KYODAN TWENTY-ONE PRECEPTS

*W*hen all human beings have accomplished the
purification of their minds and come to lead a life full
of joy, I, Tsukihi [God], will become cheered up. And
when I become cheered up, so will all human beings.
When the minds of all the world become cheered up,
God and human beings will become altogether
cheered up in one accord.

SHINTO: TENRIKYO. OFUDESAKI 7.109–11

CHAPTER SIX

Love and Service

THE SCRIPTURES OF ALL FAITHS teach that the Supreme Being is completely loving. God is all-embracing compassion. Because love is the very nature of God, we can reach God through love. Love is the quality which unites. It enables us to reach out beyond the confines of our separate egos and experience the Oneness of God.

A natural expression of love is service. By helping others we expand our love beyond ourselves, so that it takes on a more universal quality. We begin to love as God loves. In acts of service, scripture tells us, the spirit and motivation are all important. The kind of helping that is performed to merely *appear* good, or to achieve social standing, or to enhance the self in any way will only trap us in our separateness. Only service which springs spontaneously from our naturally loving soul is true spiritual service. Such humble and unaffected giving can connect us to God.

Scripture advises us to see God in those we help and to make our service an act of worship. Mother Teresa of Calcutta, a modern icon of selfless service, says that when she cares for the dying and destitute, she sees "Christ in all his distressing disguises." When we see others as a part of God, just as we are, service is as natural and unaffected as the right hand helping the left hand.

OPPOSITE
The Last Supper,
*Lucas van Leyden
(1494-1533).*

GOD IS LOVE

The New Testament states that "God is love" (1 John 4.8), a sentiment repeated in various ways by all spiritual traditions. The Aramaic Gospel of Peace of Jesus Christ adds that Mother Earth is also love, and so is the Son of Man. The Son of Man is a Jewish phrase that does not refer only to Jesus, but to human beings generally. Love is the power that unites Father, Mother, and Son together. It links spirit, matter, and humanity.

The ancient Greeks saw Eros, the god of love, as the firstborn of the gods. The Hindu Atharva Veda sees love as even higher than the gods. In the Bhagavad Gita, Krishna, who is an embodiment of the Supreme Being, declares that love is his innermost nature. The Buddhist Gandavyuha Sutra sees compassion as the essence of Buddhahood. The Mahaparinirvana Sutra states that compassion is Brahma (God) and the Tathagata (the Buddha). It is the bodhi path – the way to intuitive knowledge of truth.

My mercy embraces all things.

ISLAM: QUR'AN 7.156

*God is the great exemplar of loving
kindness. The world itself was created
solely in loving kindness.
The Lord is gracious and merciful,
slow to anger and abounding in
steadfast love. The Lord is good to all,
and his compassion is over all that he
has made.*

JUDAISM AND CHRISTIANITY: PSALMS 89.3
AND 145.8-9

*To love is to know Me, My
innermost nature, the truth that I am.*

HINDUISM: BHAGAVAD GITA 18.55

BELOW
*Camels drinking,
facsimile from
Vienna Genesis.*

*FOR YOUR HEAVENLY FATHER IS LOVE.
FOR YOUR EARTHLY MOTHER IS LOVE.
FOR THE SON OF MAN IS LOVE.*

*It is by love that the Heavenly Father and the Earthly Mother and the Son of Man
become one. For the spirit of the Son of Man was created from the spirit of the
Heavenly Father, and his body from the body of the Earthly Mother.*

CHRISTIANITY: THE GOSPEL OF PEACE OF JESUS CHRIST

RIGHT
Shakyamuni and the celestial assembly.

The Great Compassionate Heart is the essence of Buddhahood.

BUDDHISM: GANDAVYUHA SUTRA

*Love is the firstborn, loftier than the
gods, the fathers and men.
You, O Love, are the eldest of all,
altogether mighty.
To you we pay homage!
Greater than the breadth of earth
and heaven, or of waters and fire,
You, O Love, are the eldest of all,
altogether mighty.
To you we pay homage!
In many a form of goodness, O Love,
you show your face.
Grant that these forms may penetrate
within our hearts.
Send elsewhere all malice!*

HINDUISM: ATHARVA VEDA 9.2.19–25

*O good man! One who acts well,
thinks true thoughts.
True thoughts are compassion.
Compassion is the Tathagata.
O good man!
Compassion is the bodhi path;
The bodhi path is the Tathagata.
The Tathagata is compassion.
O good man!
Compassion is Great Brahma.
Great Brahma is compassion.
Compassion is the Tathagata.
O good man! Compassion acts as
parent to all beings.
The parent is compassion.
Know that compassion
is the Tathagata.
O good man! Compassion is the
Buddha nature of all beings.
Such a Buddha nature is long
overshadowed by illusion.
That is why beings cannot see.
The Buddha nature is Compassion.
Compassion is the Tathagata.*

BUDDHISM: MAHAPARINIRVANA SUTRA 259

LOVE IS THE WAY

Love is God and also the way to God. Our essential nature is love and love is the way to awaken it. The Hindu Mundaka Upanishad teaches that the self can not be known through thoughts, but only through love. To awaken this love is the goal of life. Love reveals to us a permanent truth beyond the transient nature of this world.

The Greek philosopher Plato conceived of love as a great spirit who connects humanity to God. It is the power which "prevents the universe falling into separate halves." Love unites. Without fellow feeling, the Taoist Master Chuang Tzu declares, other people will always remain strangers to us. Love makes us want to be of service, which according to Jain scripture, is a basic human function. Tenrikyo tells us that by saving others we save ourselves, because if we do not love we will be forever cut off from our self.

Bright but hidden,
the Self dwells in the heart.
Everything that moves,
breathes, opens, and closes,
lives in the Self.
He is the source of love
And may be known through love
but not through thought.
He is the goal of life.
Attain this goal!

The shining Self
dwells hidden in the heart.
Everything in the cosmos,
great and small,
lives in the Self.
He is the source of life,
Truth beyond the transience
of this world.
He is the goal of life.
Attain this goal!

HINDUISM: MUNDAKA UPANISHAD 2.2.1–2

"Look how he abused me
and beat me,
How he threw me down
and robbed me."
Live with such thoughts,
and you live in hate.

"Look how he abused me
and beat me,
How he threw me down
and robbed me."
Abandon such thoughts,
and live in love.

In this world
hate never yet dispelled hate.
Only love dispels hate.
This is the law,
Ancient and inexhaustible.

You too shall pass away.
Knowing this, how can you quarrel?

BUDDHISM: DHAMMAPADA 1

Become, perfect as the spirit of your Heavenly Father and the body of your Earthly Mother are perfect. And so love your Heavenly Father, as he loves your spirit. And so love your Earthly Mother, as she loves your body. And so love your true brothers, as your Heavenly Father and your Earthly Mother love them. And then your Heavenly Father shall give you his holy spirit, and your Earthly Mother shall give you her holy body. And then shall the Sons of Men like true brothers give love to one another; and they shall all become comforters one of another. And then shall disappear from the earth all evil and all sorrow, and there shall be love and joy upon earth. And then shall the earth be like the heavens, and the kingdom of God shall come. For love is eternal. Love is stronger than death.

CHRISTIANITY: THE GOSPEL OF PEACE OF
JESUS CHRIST

Gentle character it is which enables the rope of life to stay unbroken in one's hand.

INDIGENOUS RELIGIONS: A YORUBA PROVERB
FROM NIGERIA

See to it that whoever enters your house obtains something to eat, however little you may have. Such food will be a source of death to you if you withhold it.

INDIGENOUS RELIGIONS: A NATIVE
AMERICAN WINNEBAGO PRECEPT

Confucius said "Love men."

CONFUCIANISM: ANALECTS XII, 22

Rendering help to another is the function of all human beings.

JAINISM: TATTVARTHASUTRA 5.21

He who can find no room for others lacks fellow feeling, and to him who lacks fellow feeling, all men are strangers.

TAOISM: CHUANG TZU 23

In conflict, it is love that wins. Love is the strongest protection. If you have love, it is as if Heaven itself were keeping you safe.

TAOISM: TAO TE CHING 67

Understand that through saving others you shall also be saved.

SHINTO: TENRIKYO. OFUDESAKI 3.47

Whether you love the One or another human being, if you love enough, in the end you will come into the presence of Love itself.

ISLAM: SUFI MASTER RUMI

I teach others that human nature can find no better helper than Love. I tell you, it is every person's duty to honor Love. I especially honor and practice the mysteries of Love myself, and recommend others to do likewise. To the best of my abilities, I praise the power of and courage of Love – now and always.

ANCIENT MYSTERY RELIGIONS:
PLATO, THE SYMPOSIUM

JUDAISM ON LOVE

Jewish scripture teaches that to love God we should always act lovingly. It tells us that we should love God whether God brings us what we desire or what we hate – even death. Rabbi Yohanan ben Zakkai listens to many descriptions of the "good way," but approves the simple formula of having a good heart, for in this all other descriptions of the way are included. If the heart is open to love, it is open to God.

The scripture says "To love the Lord, your God." Whatever you do, therefore, do not do except for love.

Love God even though He kills you, for are we not taught to love God with our very soul? And what does that mean but that we are to love Him even if He takes the soul from us?

The lovers of God are of two kinds: some love Him because He gave them wealth, power and length of life. Had they lacked these they might have felt the reverse towards Him. Others love God because He is their beloved Master whether He give them good or evil.

Greater is he who acts from love than he who acts from fear.

The Holy Spirit rests on him only who has a joyous heart.

Rabbi Yohanan ben Zakkai said, "What is the good way to which a man should cleave?" Rabbi Eliezer said, "A good eye"; Rabbi Joshua said, "A good friend"; Rabbi Jose said, "A good neighbor"; Rabbi Simeon said, "One who foresees the fruit of an action"; Rabbi Elazar

said, "A good heart." Thereupon he said to them, "I approve the words of Elazar ben Arach, rather than your words, for in his words yours are included."

JUDAISM: SIFRE TO DEUT., 6,5;
INTRODUCTION TO THE ZOHAR, 12A; SOTA
31A; SUKKAT 5.1; ABOT 2.13

BELOW
The risen Christ meets Mary Magdalene.

CHRISTIANITY ON LOVE

Christ preached the way of love. In the New Testament the disciple John tells us that God is love and without love we may not know God. Through loving others we can experience that He has given us his spirit – that God lives in us and we live in God. If we cannot love our fellow humans whom we can see, John asks, how can we ever begin to love the invisible God?

In his beautiful letter to the Corinthians, St. Paul eulogizes love as the greatest of all qualities. Spiritual powers, great knowledge, sacrifice, and the faith to move mountains are all of no value compared to love. All such things are imperfect and will pass away, but love alone is perfect and enduring. Only love truly connects us to God.

Beloved, let us love one another; for love is of God, and he who loves is born of God and knows God. He who does not love does not know God; for God is love.

No man has ever seen God, yet if we love one another, God abides in us and his love is perfected in us. By this we know that we live in him and he in us, because he has given us of his own Spirit.

There is no fear in love, for perfect love casts out fear. Fear has to do with punishment, and he who fears is not perfected in love. We love, because he first loved us. If anyone says, "I love God," and hates his brother, he is a liar; for he who does not love his brother whom he has seen, cannot love God whom he has not seen.

CHRISTIANITY: I JOHN 4.7-20

If I speak in the tongues of men and of angels, but have not love, I am a noisy gong or a clanging cymbal. And if I have prophetic powers, and understand all mysteries and all knowledge, and if I have the faith to move mountains, but have not love, I am nothing. If I give away all I have, and if I give my body to be burned, but have not love, I gain nothing.

Love is patient and kind; love is not jealous or boastful; it is not arrogant or rude. Love does not insist on its own way; it is not irritable or resentful; it does not rejoice at wrong, but rejoices in the right. Love bears all things, believes all things, hopes all things, endures all things.

Love never ends. As for prophecies, they will be fulfilled; as for tongues, they will cease; as for knowledge, it will be surpassed. Our knowledge is imperfect and our prophecy is incomplete; but when the perfect comes, the imperfect will pass away. When I was a child, I spoke like a child, I thought like a child, I reasoned like a child. But when I became a man, I gave up childish ways. Now we see in a mirror dimly, but we will see face to face. Now I know in part, but I will understand fully, just as I have been fully understood. So, in this life there are only three lasting qualities – faith, hope, and love – the greatest of which is love.

CHRISTIANITY: 1 CORINTHIANS 13

BAHA'I ON LOVE

The Baha'i faith is a relatively new, but already widespread faith. It was founded in Persia by Baha'u'llah (1817–92), who is seen as the latest in a succession of prophets. He was regarded as a threat by the religious authorities who repeatedly imprisoned and exiled him. Many of his followers were put to death. Baha'u'llah called for all religions to return to their true spiritual intent of furthering "knowledge of God" and "unity and fellowship." He sees all spiritual traditions as essentially united within God's love. Love can overcome religious fanaticism and help all faiths to realize that they are different fruits from one tree. Love is the power that can clean the mirror of the heart so that it reflects the universal divine light.

O my brother! A pure heart is as a mirror; cleanse it with the burnish of love and severance from all save God, that the true sun may shine within it and the eternal morning dawn.

BAHA'I FAITH: THE SEVEN VALLEYS AND THE FOUR VALLEYS 21

BELOW
The Maqamat of al-Kasim, *B. Ali al Harin (de. 516)*

Strengthen your endeavor, O people of Baha, that the tumult of religious dissension and strife that agitates the peoples of the earth may he stilled, that every trace of it may be completely obliterated. For the love of God, and them that serve Him, arise to aid this sublime and momentous Revelation. Religious fanaticism and hatred are a world-devouring fire, whose violence none can quench. Only the hand of divine power can deliver mankind from this desolating affliction. The utterance of God is a lamp, whose light are these words: You are the fruits of one tree, and the leaves of one branch. Deal with one another with the utmost love and harmony, with friendliness and fellowship. He who is the day-star of truth bears me witness! So powerful is the light of unity that it can illuminate the whole earth. The One true God who knows all things, Himself testifies to the truth of these words.

BAHA'I FAITH: EPISTLE TO THE SON OF THE WOLF

HINDUISM ON SERVICE

Love is more than just a feeling. It informs and motivates action. Service of others is love in action. It is a practical demonstration of our ability to cast off the confines of selfishness and sense our unity with others. When we are in touch with our essential nature, the sufferings of others awakens love within us, and service is the natural response.

In the Hindu Bhagavad Gita, Krishna teaches his disciple Arjuna the power of selfless service. Paradoxically, through selflessness we find the fulfillment of our desires. By abandoning our obsession with own needs and pleasures, in favor of serving others, we can refind our eternal home. Those who have no selfish concern for the fruits of their actions, but offer all their work up to God, become free and secure. If we fail to serve others, however, our lives will have been wasted.

Selfless service is a path to realizing the Oneness of Brahman (God). Every selfless act comes from God, because in it there is no sense of a separate doer. God's servant knows that it is not he who acts, but God through him. Everything is God, including the servant and those he serves.

At the beginning, mankind and the obligation of selfless service were created together. "Through selfless service, you will always be fruitful and find the fulfillment of your desires:" this is the promise of the Creator.

Every selfless act, Arjuna, is born from Brahman, the eternal, infinite Godhead. He is present in every act of service. All life turns on this law, O Arjuna. Whoever violates it, indulging his senses for his own pleasure and ignoring the needs of others, has wasted his life. But those who realize the Self are always satisfied. Having found the source of joy and fulfillment they no longer seek happiness from the external world. They have nothing to gain or lose by any action; neither people nor things can affect their security.

Strive constantly to serve the welfare of the world; by devotion to selfless work one attains the supreme goal of life. Do your work with the welfare of others always in mind.

True sustenance is in service, and through it a man or woman reaches the eternal Brahman. But those who do not seek to serve are without a home in this world. Arjuna, how can they be at home in any world to come?

HINDUISM: BHAGAVAD GITA, CHS 3 AND 4

BELOW
The Submission of Kaliya, *Basohli (1700-65).*

BUDDHISM ON SERVICE

Buddhism teaches that we should have compassion for all sentient beings. Unlike most people who looks after "number one," and maybe their immediate friends and family, an enlightened being nourishes all people. According to the Dhammapada, encountering those in need is not a burden but a sweetness. It is an opportunity to share happiness and do something good before leaving this transitory life.

If beings knew, as I know, the fruit of sharing gifts, they would not enjoy their use without sharing them, nor would the taint of stinginess obsess the heart and stay there. Even if it were their last morsel of food, they would not enjoy its use without sharing it, if there were anyone to receive it.

There are three kinds of persons existing in the world: one is like a drought, one like local rainfall, and one like rain that pours down everywhere. How is a person like a drought? He gives nothing to all alike. In this way, a person is like a drought. How is a person like a local rainfall? He is a giver to some, but to others he gives not. In this way, a person is like a local rainfall. How does a person rain down everywhere? He gives to all. In this way a person rains down everywhere.

BUDDHISM: ITIVUTTAKA 18 AND 65

*To have friends in need is sweet
And to share happiness.
And to have done something good
Before leaving this life is sweet,
And to let go of sorrow.*

BUDDHISM: DHAMMAPADA 23

BELOW
Thanka showing incarnations of the Buddha, Tibetan, 19th century.

JUDAISM ON SERVICE

Jewish scripture teaches that we are all responsible for each other. Even those with little should still find something to give to others. Deeds of loving kindness are equal to all of the words of the commandments, and one who does not perform kind acts does not know God. God loves those who love others, and someone who prays for others will be answered before one who prays first for himself. A poor man is a gift from God, because through easing his poverty we may win God's grace.

The Book of the Secrets of Enoch, a mysterious Jewish work attributed to the Old Testament prophet, teaches us to help others in affliction so that we will not be so afflicted ourselves. In a delightful Jewish story the great prophet Elijah appears to Rabbi Barucha and can find only two people in the marketplace worthy of a share in the world to come – two clowns who cheer up those who are sad and heal the divisions between those who are quarreling.

All men are responsible for one another.
Even a poor man who himself subsists on charity should give charity.
He who prays for his fellowman, while he himself has the same need, will be answered first.
Deeds of kindness are equal in weight to all the commandments.
He who does not perform deeds of loving-kindness is as one who has no God.
When the Holy One loves a man, He sends him a present in the shape of a poor man, so that he should perform some good deed to him, through the merit of which he may draw to himself a cord of grace.

JUDAISM: SANHEDRIN 27B; GITTIN 7B; BABA KAMMA 92A; Y. PEAH, 1, 1; ABODAH ZARAH, 17B ; ZOHAR, GENESIS 104A

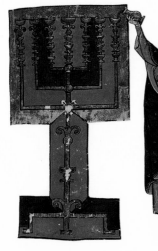

BELOW
Hebrew biblical text showing a man pouring oil into candlesticks, 13th century.

Stretch out your hands to the poor according to your strength. Do not hide your silver in the earth. Help the faithful man in affliction and affliction will not find you in the time of your trouble. And every grievous and cruel yoke that comes upon you, bear all for the sake of the Lord, and thus you will find your reward in the day of judgment.

JUDAISM: THE BOOK OF THE SECRETS OF ENOCH

Rabbi Barucha of Huza often went to the marketplace at Lapet. One day, the prophet Elijah appeared to him there, and Rabbi Barucha asked him, "Is there anyone among all these people who will have a share in the World to Come?" Elijah answered, "There is none." Later, two men came to the marketplace, and Elijah said to Rabbi Barucha, "Those two will have a share in the World to Come!" Rabbi Barucha asked the newcomers, "What is your occupation?" They replied, "We are clowns. When we see someone who is sad, we cheer him up. When we see two people quarreling, we try to make peace between them."

JUDAISM: TAANIT 22A

CHRISTIANITY ON SERVICE

Christian scripture teaches that giving is better than receiving. Giving frees us from the separate self, while receiving may bind us more tightly to it. In the Gnostic Gospel of Thomas, Jesus advises us not to lend our money at interest, but to give it away without any expectation of return. In the Gospel of John, Jesus washes his disciples' feet, giving a practical demonstration of the spirit of humble service he wishes to impart to them.

Jewish scripture teaches "Love your neighbor as yourself." In the famous Parable of the Good Samaritan, Jesus shows that we should not interpret the word *neighbor* in a local or even national way, but widen it to include all humankind. In the Parable of the Sheep and Goats, Jesus paints a picture of the Day of Judgment in which the Son of Man puts the righteous at his right hand and the unrighteous at his left hand. He praises those who served others and condemns those who did not. God is in all of us. When we help the needy, we are helping God. If we do not, we are allowing God to suffer. What we do to others, we do to God.

It is more blessed to give than to receive.

CHRISTIANITY: ACTS 20.35

Do not neglect to show hospitality to strangers, for thereby some have entertained angels unawares.

CHRISTIANITY: HEBREWS 13.2

Whatever you do, do it to the glory of God.

CHRISTIANITY: 1 CORINTHIANS 10.31

Jesus said "If you have money, do not lend it at interest, but give to one from whom you will not get it back."

CHRISTIANITY: THE GOSPEL OF THOMAS 95

When Jesus had washed their feet, he took his garments and resumed his place, saying to them, "Do you see what I have just done for you? You call me Teacher and Master, and you are right, for that is what I am. If I, your Master and Teacher, have washed your feet, you also ought to wash one another's feet. For I have given you an example and you should follow it."

CHRISTIANITY: JOHN 13.12-17

BELOW
Christ and the Samaritan Woman, *Bernardo Strozzi (1581-1644).*

An expert in the Law stood up to test Jesus. He asked, "Teacher, what should I do to be sure of eternal life?" Jesus replied by asking him, "What is written in the Law? How do you read it?" And he answered, "You shall love the Lord your God with all your heart, and with all your soul, and with all your strength, and with all your mind; and your neighbor as yourself." And Jesus said to him, "That's right. Do this, and you will live."

But the lawyer, wanting to justify himself, continued, "But who is my neighbor?" Jesus replied, "A man was traveling from Jerusalem to Jericho, and he was attacked by thieves who beat him, and left him half-dead. Now, by chance, a priest was going down that road and when he saw him he passed by on the other side. A Levite also came along, but also passed by on the other side. However, a Samaritan happened upon him and compassionately went to him and bound up his wounds, pouring on oil and wine. Then he put him on his own mule and took him to an inn, where he took care of him. The next day he gave two denarii to the innkeeper, saying, 'Look after him. If this is not enough I will repay you when I come back.' Which of these three, do you think, proved to be a neighbor to the man attacked by thieves?" The lawyer replied, "The one who showed mercy to him." And Jesus said "Go, and do likewise."

CHRISTIANITY: LUKE 10.25–37

Then the King will say to those at his right hand, "Blessed of my Father, come and inherit the kingdom prepared for you from the foundation of the world; for I was hungry and you fed me, I was thirsty and you gave me drink, I was a stranger and you welcomed me, I was naked and you clothed me, I was sick and you visited me, I was in prison and you came to me."

Then the righteous will answer him, "Lord, when did we do these things?"

And the King will answer, "What you did for the least of these my brethren, you did to me."

Then he will say to those at his left hand, "Leave me, you are cursed to enter the eternal fire prepared for the devil and his angels; for I was hungry and you gave me no food, I was thirsty and you gave me no drink, I was a stranger and you did not welcome me, naked and you did not clothe me, sick and in prison and you did not visit me."

Then they also will answer, "Lord, when did we not do these things?" And he will answer "What you did not do for the least of these, you did not do for me." And they will go away into eternal punishment, while the righteous enjoy eternal life.

CHRISTIANITY: MATTHEW 25.31–46

ISLAM ON SERVICE

The Qur'an teaches that true piety lies not in outer religious observances, but in belief in God and sharing what one has with the needy; serving others for love of God and seeking no reward for ourselves. In the Hadith, Muhammad teaches that we should help everyone – both oppressor and oppressed. How should we help the oppressor? By hindering him doing wrong, Muhammad explains.

This advice is a profound teaching on how to deal with the perpetrators of injustice. Muhammad is not advising us to ignore their crimes but to oppose the oppressor in a spirit of loving service, not in a spirit of enmity. The oppressor is suffering in his own way, whether he recognizes it or not. It is to the benefit of all that oppression ceases. By approaching the unjust in this way, we avoid exiling them from our hearts and perpetuating the separateness in which they are trapped. We allow them the opportunity to realize the error of their ways and awaken their own innate goodness.

They feed with food the needy wretch, the orphan, and the prisoner, for love of Him, saying, "We wish for no reward nor thanks from you."

ISLAM: QUR'AN 76.8–9

According to Anas ibn Malik, the Prophet said, "Help your brother whether he is oppressor or oppressed." Anas replied to him, "O Messenger of God, a man who is oppressed I am ready to help, but how does one help an oppressor?" "By hindering him doing wrong," he said.

ISLAM: HADITH OF BUKHARI

It is not piety that you turn your faces in prayer to the East and to the West. True piety is this: to believe in God, and the Last Day, the angels, the Book, and the Prophets, to give of one's goods, however cherished, to kinsmen, and orphans, the needy, the traveler, beggars, and to ransom the slave, to perform the prayer, to pay the alms.

And they who fulfill their covenant, when they have engaged in a covenant, and endure with fortitude misfortune, hardship, and peril, these are they who are true in their faith, and truly in awe of God.

ISLAM: QUR'AN 2.177

BELOW
Muhammad delivering his last sermon in the Madinah Mosque, Mecca, Turkish, 18th century.

COMPASSION FOR ALL LIVING BEINGS

Jain scripture teaches us to love and serve all sentient beings who experience pain and fear just as we do. Jains wear masks and brush the street under their feet to avoid inadvertently inhaling or crushing small insects. Jainism teaches that we should not harm even earth, water, fire, and air – all of which are full of life. The unenlightened, suffering from the karma of their previous bad actions, continue to cause much pain in a world already rife with suffering. The true sage who understands karma has respect for all life. Those whose minds are at peace and who are free from passions do not desire to live at the expense of others.

The Taoist Tract of the Quiet Way advises freeing captive animals. The Gospel of Peace of Jesus Christ sees animals and humans as sharing one earthly mother, and therefore sees the butchering of animals as the murder of our brothers. The Buddhist sage Milarepa wishes that not even insects be bound to the illusion of *samsara*, the cycle of uncontrolled rebirth. The Khuddaka Patha recommends all-embracing thoughts for all that lives. In the Hadith, Muhammad relates that God pardoned a man his sins because of the kindness he showed to a thirsty dog, affirming, "There will be a reward for anyone who gives water to a being that has a tender heart."

Buy captive animals
and give them freedom.
How commendable is abstinence
that dispenses with the butcher!
While walking be mindful
of worms and ants.
Be cautious with fire and do not set
mountain woods or forests ablaze.
Do not go into the mountain
to catch birds in nets,
nor to the water to poison fishes
and minnows.
Do not butcher the ox
that plows your field.

TAOISM: TRACT OF
THE QUIET WAY

May no living creatures,
not even insects,
Be bound unto samsaric life;
nay, not one of them;
But may I be empowered
to save them all.

BUDDHISM: MILAREPA

As a mother with her own life guards
the life of her child,
have all-embracing thoughts
for all that lives.

BUDDHISM: KHUDDAKA PATHA, METTA
SUTTA

It was said to them of old time,
"Honor your Heavenly Father and
your Earthly Mother, and do their
commandments, that your days may
be long upon the earth." And next
afterward was given this
commandment, "You shall not kill."
For life is given to all by God, and
that which God has given, let not
man take away. For I tell you truly,
from one Mother proceeds all that
lives upon the earth. Therefore, he
who kills, kills his brother. And from
him will the Earthly Mother turn
away, and will pluck from him her
quickening breasts. And he will be
shunned by her angels, and Satan
will have his dwelling in his body.
And the flesh of slain beasts in his
body will become his own tomb. For
I tell you truly, he who kills, kills
himself, and whoso eats the flesh of
slain beasts, eats of the body of death.
For in his blood every drop of their
blood turns to poison. And their
death will become his death.

CHRISTIANITY: THE GOSPEL OF PEACE OF
JESUS CHRIST

According to Abu Hurairah, the
Messenger of God said, "A man
traveling along a road felt extremely
thirsty and went down a well and
drank. When he came up he saw a
dog panting with thirst and licking
the moist earth. 'This animal,' the
man said, 'is suffering from thirst just
as much as I was.' So he went down
the well again, filled his shoe with
water, and taking it in his teeth
climbed out of the well and gave the
water to the dog. God was pleased
with his act and granted him pardon
for his sins."

Someone said, "O Messenger of God,
will we then have a reward for the
good done to our animals?" "There
will be a reward," he replied, "for
anyone who gives water to a being
that has a tender heart."

ISLAM: HADITH OF BUKHARI

RIGHT
*The exodus from
Noah's ark and
drunkenness of
Noah,* Bedford
Book of Hours,
French, c. 1423.

All sentient beings experience pleasure and displeasure – pain, terror and sorrow. They all are filled with fear, coming from every directions. Despite this, some people exist who cause greater pain to them. Some kill animals for sacrifice, or for their skin, flesh, blood, feathers, teeth, and tusks; some kill them intentionally and some unintentionally; some kill because they have been previously injured by them, and some because they expect to be injured. Someone who harms an animal has not understood or renounced misguided deeds. Someone who knows the nature of sin against animals is called a true sage, who understands karma, Unenlightened men, who suffer from the effects of past deeds, cause great suffering in a world already full of suffering. Many souls are individually embodied in earth. Therefore, if desiring to gain praise, honour, respect, to achieve a good rebirth, to achieve liberation, or to avoid pain, a man sins against earth or causes or permits others to do so, he will not gain joy or wisdom. Injuring earth is like striking, cutting, maiming, or killing a blind man. Understanding this, people should not sin against earth or cause or permit others to do so. He who knows the nature of sin against earth is called a true sage who understands karma.

There are also many souls embodied in water. Water is alive. Someone who injures the lives in water does not understand or renounce sin. Knowing this, a man should not sin against water, or cause or permit others to do so. He who knows the nature of sin against water is called a true sage who understands karma.

With malicious or thoughtless acts one may destroy fire-beings, and moreover, harm other beings with fire. For there are creatures living in earth, grass, leaves, wood, cow dung, or dust heaps, and jumping creatures which fall into a fire if they come near it. If touched by fire, they shrivel up, lose their senses, and die. He who knows the nature of sin against and with fire is called a true sage who understands karma.

Someone who doesn't even want to harm the wind knows the sufferings of all living things. He who knows what is bad for himself knows what is bad for others, and he who knows what is bad for others knows what is bad for himself. This reciprocity should always be borne in mind. Those whose minds are at peace and who are free from passions do not desire to live at the expense of others. He who understands the nature of sin against wind is called a true sage who understands karma.

JAINISM: ACARANGA-SUTRA 1,1

LOVE IN ACTION

From a spiritual perspective, the value of service lies not so much in the act performed, but in the selfless intention from which it comes. Service must be love in action, not a heartless formality or social convention. The Buddhist Precious Garland scripture says that no amount of empty service rivals the value of an instant of genuine love. Jewish scripture remarks that a smile is worth more than offering milk to the thirsty. Essentially, service is about sharing love, which is the most fundamental of all human needs. Without this vital ingredient, helping does not go to the heart of things. However, it is better to act kindly with an ulterior motive than not at all, for through so doing, we may begin to acquire the habit which will, in time, lead to right motivation.

Christ advises "do not let your left hand know what your right hand is doing." Ideally we should act with humble anonymity, seeking no reward or recognition for our kindness, which will only aggrandize the self. The Tao Te Ching teaches us to let go of our ideas about how we think things should be and allow service to arise spontaneously from the natural goodness of our essential being. This innate empathy, says Jain scripture, is the source of all virtue. The Guide to the Bodhisattva's Way of Life, a central Mahayana Buddhist text, reminds us of our essential unity – we are all limbs of one life. Helping others, therefore, should be as obvious and uncomplicated as feeding ourselves.

The whole worth of a benevolent deed lies in the love that inspires it.

JUDAISM: SUKKAH, 49B

Better he who shows a smiling countenance than him who offers milk to drink.

JUDAISM: KETUBOT, 111

Engage in Torah and charity even with an ulterior motive, for the habit of right doing will lead also to right motivation.

JUDAISM: PESAHIM 50B

Those who serve God from love will be like servants who lay out gardens and delights with which to please their absent lord when he returns.

JUDAISM: TANA D'BE ELIYAHU, 560

RIGHT
St. Christopher bears Christ over the river, Book of Hours, *French, 15th century.*

When you give alms, do not let your left hand know what your right hand is doing.

CHRISTIANITY: MATTHEW 6.3

*When being of service
or caring for others,
don't overdo it.
Meaning – let go of your ideas
about how it should be.
Natural Goodness is like a deep well
inside of you.
If you have been drawing
from this well,
then nothing is impossible.
There are no limits
to what you can achieve,
and you are able to truly help.
Be like a mother;
and the effects of what you do
will last.
Have deep roots in Tao.
See the eternal
beyond the impermanent.*

TAOISM: TAO TE CHING 59

*Charity – to be moved at the sight of
the thirsty, the hungry, and the
miserable and to offer relief to them
out of pity – is the spring of virtue.*

JAINISM: KUNDAKUNDA, PANCASTIKAYA 137

*Even three times a day to offer
Three hundred cooking pots of food
Does not match a portion of the merit
Acquired in one instant of love.*

BUDDHISM: NAGARJUNA, PRECIOUS
GARLAND 283

*Why should I be unable
To regard the bodies of others as "I?"
It is not difficult to see
that my body is also that of others.
In the same way as the hands
and so forth
are regarded as limbs of the body,
likewise why are embodied creatures
not regarded as limbs of life?
Only through acquaintance has the
thought of "I" arisen
towards this impersonal body;
so in a similar way,
why should it not arise
towards other living beings?
When I work in this way
for the sake of others,
I should not let conceit or the feeling
that I am wonderful arise.
It is just like feeding myself –
hoping for nothing in return.*

BUDDHISM. SHANTIDEVA, GUIDE TO THE
BODHISATTVA'S WAY OF LIFE 8.112–16

CHAPTER SEVEN

Devotion and Worship

MOST RELIGIOUS TRADITIONS practice some type of worship of the Supreme Being. Sometimes the Supreme Being is envisioned as a mighty king before whom we bow in humility, sometimes as a loving father or mother whom we should honor and obey, and sometimes as an intimate friend or lover with whom we can play and delight. All these approaches give the ineffable Oneness a human face so that we can approach the divine in a human way.

From a spiritual perspective, worship and devotion are not performed for God's benefit, but for ours. God is whole and perfect and does not need our praise and approval. Worship is a way of remembering the sacredness of life and of affirming our connection to God. Chanting, singing, repeating liturgy, bowing before icons, performing rituals, and offering prayers can all have a profound effect upon practitioners. They alter their state of consciousness and open them to the inner self. The scriptures teach that the most important thing is not the form that worship takes, but the sincerity with which it is entered into. Only if devotion genuinely expresses love for God will it help us to reach him.

OPPOSITE
Celebration of the end of Ramadan, from "The Maqamat," Persian.

ويحك القفص والجبال والفرس والابلة انها لضغت على بالله فانضاعت نقض من رجها

فنشد مزرجها فلما داننى وقفت بالرقعة درهما وقطعه وقلت لها ان رغبت فى المشوف المعلم

واشرت الى الجب الدرهم فوجى بالسر المدهم وان ابنت نسرجى فخذى القطعة وآبيرجن

قالت الى اسنلاص البدر النم والابلج الهم وقالت دع جدلك وينلع عما بدلك فاسطن

طلع الشيخ وبلدنه والشعر وايبج بردنه فقلن ان الشيخ من اهل سروج وهو الذى وثن

DEVOTION TO GOD

Devotion to God is a way of purification. God is goodness and truth, and our love of him frees us from evil and falsehood. Devotion is a path of the heart. It is not about philosophy or trying to make sense of things. It is entering a love affair with life, which may be as crazy and irrational as any other emotional involvement. Through worshiping God, devotees may enter ecstatic states of joy and rapture. As our Self awakens, we are awed by the reality of the Supreme Being toward which we have turned our heart.

*Filth on hands, feet, and body
may be washed off with water;
Clothes fouled by dirt
may be washed with soap;
The mind fouled by sin and evil
may only be cleansed
by devotion to God.*

SIKHISM: ADI GRANTH, JAPUJI 20, M.1

RIGHT
Worshiping Kuan Yin, the goddess of mercy.

He who loves me is made pure; his heart melts in joy. He rises to transcendental consciousness by the rousing of his higher emotional nature. Tears of joy flow from his eyes, his hair stands on end, his heart melts in love. The bliss in that state is so intense that, forgetful of himself and his surroundings, he sometimes weeps profusely, or laughs, or sings, or dances; such a devotee is a purifying influence upon the whole universe.

HINDUISM: SRIMAD BHAGAVATAM 11.8

*Holy is the man of devotion;
Through thoughts
and words and deed
and through his conscience
he increases Goodness;
The Wise Lord as Good Mind
is all-powerful.
For his good reward I pray.
I know that my greatest good
is to worship the Wise Lord
and those that have been and are.
By their names will I worship them
and come before them with praise.*

ZOROASTRIANISM: AVESTA, YASNA 51.21–22

LEFT
Guanyin being worshiped by the painting's donor, Chinese, 10th century.

PRAYER

Prayer is one of the most common forms of devotion. By giving thanks for what we have and affirming the goodness we wish to witness, we mysteriously call forth the grace to help goodness manifest in our lives. Prayers express a yearning for God. The Hindu Basavanna and Jewish Psalms are filled with the poignant sadness of holy longing. They poetically entice God to grace us with the knowledge of his loving presence and fill our hearts with the joy of communion. Ultimately prayer is merging the mind with God. The Christian mystic Hildegard of Bingen describes it as "breathing in and breathing out the one breath of the universe."

As a hart longs for flowing streams,
so longs my soul for you, O God.
My soul thirsts for God,
for the living God.
When shall I come and behold
the face of God?
My tears have been my food
day and night.

JUDAISM AND CHRISTIANITY: PSALM 42.1–3

Peace be to earth and to airy spaces.
Peace be to heaven,
peace to the waters,
Peace to the plants
and peace to the trees!
May all the gods grant me peace!
By this invocation of peace
may peace be diffused!
By this invocation of peace
may peace bring peace!
With this peace
the dreadful I appease,
With this peace the cruel I appease,
With this peace all evil I appease,
So that peace may prevail,
happiness prevail!
May everything for us be peaceful!

HINDUISM: ATHARVA VEDA 19.9.14 P.395

May generosity triumph
over niggardliness,
May love triumph over contempt,
May the true-spoken word triumph
over the false-spoken word,
May truth triumph over illusion.

ZOROASTRIANISM: YASNA 60.5

It is good to go morning, midday, and
evening into the Lord's dwelling, for
the glory of your creator. Every
breathing thing glorifies him, and
every creature visible and invisible
returns him praise.

JUDAISM: THE BOOK OF THE SECRETS OF
ENOCH

The chakora bird
longs for the moonlight.
The lotus longs for sunrise.
The bee longs
to drink the flower's nectar,
Even so my heart anxiously longs
for you, O Lord.

HINDUISM: BASAVANNA, VACANA 364

ABOVE
Muhammad leading
Muslims at prayer at
Kabah, Turkish.

THE LORD'S PRAYER

In the Gospel of Matthew, Jesus teaches his disciples the Lord's Prayer. The most familiar translation of this prayer is the version from the King James Bible, based on the Greek New Testament. However, Neil Douglas-Klotz has shown that the Greek gospels have already lost many levels of meaning contained in this famous prayer. For his translations he returns to the Peshitta Gospels. *Peshitta* means "simple, sincere, true, unadulterated." These Aramaic texts are regarded by Syrian and Assyrian Orthodox Christians as the oldest and most authoritative versions of the gospels. Aramaic is certainly the language that Jesus himself would have spoken. In his book *Prayers of the Cosmos,* Douglas-Klotz devotes a whole page to the many meanings conveyed by each line of the Lord's Prayer. He brings to life the deeply mystical nature of an overfamiliar scripture and presents startling evidence of how much meaning can be lost in superficial translations. Here are both the traditional King James version of the Lord's Prayer and a new version, based on some of the meanings of the original Aramaic.

Our Father which art in heaven
Hallowed be thy name.
Thy kingdom come.
Thy will be done in earth, as it is in
    heaven.
Give us this day our daily bread.
And forgive us our debts, as we
    forgive our debtors.
And lead us not into temptation, but
    deliver us from evil.
For thine is the kingdom, and the
    power, and the glory, for ever.
Amen.

CHRISTIANITY: MATTHEW 6:9–13 KING JAMES VERSION

Father-Mother!
    Birther and Breath of All.
Create a space inside us
    and fill it with your presence.
Let Oneness now prevail.
Your one desire then acts through
    ours, as energy fills all forms.
Give us physical and spiritual
    nourishment each day.
Untangle the knots of error that
    bind us, as we release others.
Don't let appearances make us
    forgetful of the Source, but free us
    to act appropriately.
Age to age, from you comes the
    glorious harmony of Life.
May these statements be fertile
    ground from which our future
    grows.

CHRISTIANITY: MATTHEW 6:9–13 NEW VERSION FROM THE ARAMAIC

GOD'S DRUNKEN LOVERS

Mystical poets often relate to God as their Beloved; turning to the imagery of romantic love and intoxication to express their ecstatic devotion. The Hindu mystic Mirabai was a woman possessed by ecstatic love for a God who responded to reckless passion not pious reverence. She danced in the temples, singing her frenzied love songs of erotic yearning and spiritual passion. She called her Beloved the "Dark One." Such imagery is also found amongst the Islamic Sufis, who are famous for their devotional poetry; as well as in the biblical poems attributed to King Solomon, called the Song of Songs.

Hurry to my bed,
covered in fresh flowers;
my body smells sweet,
ready for you.
I am your slave,
spending life after life,
making love with you only –
Mira's love-lord who never dies.
"Dark One! Give me just one
*   glimpse."*
This is all she prays.

HINDUISM: MIRABAI

My God, here I am –
consumed in your Light,
becoming a spectrum of rays from the
*   Essence,*
splashing the horizon.
Every atom in me longed for a vision,
until I collapsed drunk on your
*   manifestations.*

ISLAM: NAWAZ

Heart broken in two –
I am separate
from my lover.
Days without comfort.
Nights without sleep.
Can you comprehend this longing?
Love is absent.
The dark hours wander aimlessly.
I start up –
trembling all over with fear.
Kabir says: "Listen to me.
Only the Lover can satisfy you."

ISLAM AND HINDUISM: KABIR

O for your kiss! For your love,
More enticing than wine,
For your scent and sweet name –
For all this they love you.
Take me away to your room,
Like a king to his rooms –
We'll rejoice there with wine.
No wonder they love you!

JUDAISM AND CHRISTIANITY: THE SONG OF
SONGS 1

PRAISING MOTHER EARTH

Ancient pagan religions, indigenous religions, and many other traditions, do not only worship a transcendental God. They also praise nature, often personified as Mother Earth. Our word *matter* comes from the word for "mother." Spirit is God the Father and matter is God the Mother. The relationship between them produces life, just as the lovemaking between a man and a woman produces a child.

Behold!
Our Mother Earth is lying here.
Behold! She gives of her fruitfulness.
Truly, her power gives she us.
Give thanks to Mother Earth
who lies here.
Behold on Mother Earth
the growing fields!
Behold the promise
of her fruitfulness!
Truly, her power gives she us.
Give thanks to Mother Earth
who lies here.
Behold on Mother Earth
the spreading trees!
Behold the promise
of her fruitfulness!

Truly, her power gives she us.
Give thanks to Mother Earth
who lies here.
We see on Mother Earth
the running streams;
We see the promise of her fruitfulness.
Truly, her power gives she us.
Our thanks to Mother Earth
who lies here!

INDIGENOUS RELIGIONS: NATIVE AMERICAN
PAWNEE HYMN

LEFT
Bronze portal showing the mother goddess Thalassa or Asherah and Gaia suckling their children, Italian.

IN PRAISE OF MY SELF

The highest revelation of Hinduism is that Atman is Brahman – the Self is
God. In this extraordinary extract from the Ashtavakra Gita, the writer is
overcome by wonder at his own essential nature. This hymn to the Self does
not celebrate the personal self that lives and dies, but the immortal and
unchanging consciousness which inhabits it. The writer has become aware
that consciousness is impersonal and transcendental. It is a vast sea of being
within which individual selves arise and die like waves on a sea. It is God.

*O wonder that I am! I salute Myself
who knows no decay and survives
even the destruction of the entire
universe from the creator Brahma to
a blade of grass.*

*O, the wonder that I am! I salute
Myself who, though with a body, am
one who neither goes anywhere nor
comes from anywhere but ever abides
pervading the universe.*

*O, in Me, the limitless ocean, the
movement in the mind has produced
the many worlds like the wind
produces diverse waves on the ocean.
How remarkable! In Me the limitless
ocean, the waves of individual selves
arise according to their inherent
nature, meet and play with one
another for a while and then
disappear.*

HINDUISM: ASHTAVAKRA GITA 31–45

LEFT
*Krishna, from the
Hindu epic, the
Adhyatma
Ramayana, by a
Chapra artist.*

Devotion to the Master

Devotion is often expressed towards a spiritual master who has the power to reveal God to his or her devotees. If the master has become enlightened and has realized his oneness with all things, he is regarded in some traditions as an embodiment of God, and worship of the master is worship of God. In the Hindu tradition, certain teachers are termed *avatars*. Such beings are not ordinary humans who have searched for and found God. They are born with complete knowledge of God. They are God incarnate. Whereas most of us have come here to learn, they have come to grace us with their divine presence.

One such incarnation is Krishna. As well as being the awesome teacher in the Bhagavad Gita, he is a delightfully playful figure who dances and plays the flute. He is pictured surrounded by shepherd girls who are his devotees. He tests their devotion by encouraging them to leave him, but they will not be sent away. To their delight, the blissful Krishna then divides himself into many forms so that he can seem to dance with each of his loves. This is a beautiful metaphor of God's relationship with the soul. Although we are many, God seems to have a personal and intimate relationship with each one of us. Through this sacred dance of love we may realize that our true relationship with God is more intimate still – we are Krishna.

Jesus Christ is believed by Christians to be an incarnation of God. In the Gospel of Mark a woman shows her devotion by anointing Jesus with expensive oils. Some of his followers are angry that the oil was not sold and the money given to the poor, in the spirit of Christ's teachings. But Jesus reprimands them. He accepts the woman's devotion without criticism. There will always be the poor to serve, but there is not always a living master to honor and adore.

When Jesus was sitting at a table in the house of Simon the leper at Bethany, a woman approached with an alabaster flask full of expensive ointment, which she broke and poured the contents over his head. Some muttered indignantly to themselves and reproached the woman, saying, "Why have you wasted this ointment? It could have been sold for more than three hundred denarii, and the money given to the poor." But Jesus said, "Leave her alone. Why are you bothering her? She has done a beautiful thing for me. You will always have the poor with you, and whenever you wish, you can help them; but you will not always have me."

Christianity: Mark 14.3–9

LEFT
Christ washing the disciples' feet, from The Hasting Hours.

LEFT
*Krishna
celebrating the
festival of Holi,
Indian,
c. 1775-80.*

*To the shepherd girls, Krishna was
their beloved friend, lover, and
companion. When Sri Krishna played
on his flute, the shepherd girls forgot
everything; unconscious even of their
own bodies, they ran to him, drawn
by his great love. Once Krishna, to
test their devotion to him, said to
them, "O you pure ones, your duties
must be first to your husbands and
children. Go back to your homes and
live in their service. You need not
come to me. You need only meditate
on me to gain salvation." But the
shepherd girls replied, "O you cruel
lover, we desire to serve only you!
You know the scriptural truths, and
advise us to serve our husbands and
children. Very well; we shall abide by
your teaching. Since you are all in all,
and are all, by serving you we shall
be serving them also."*

*Krishna, who gives delight to all
and who is blissful in his own being,
divided himself into as many
Krishnas as there were shepherd girls,
and danced and played with them.
Each girl felt the divine presence and
divine love of Sri Krishna. Each felt
herself the most blessed. Each one's
love for Krishna was so absorbing
that she felt herself one with Krishna
– indeed, knew herself to be Krishna.*

HINDUISM: SRIMAD BHAGAVATAM 10.5

INNER SINCERITY

From a spiritual perspective, the most important thing in acts of worship and devotion is the inner sincerity of the devotee. This alone will help us open our heart to God. The Talmud relates that King David became proud of the devotional psalms which he had composed. God humbled him, however, by sending a simple frog who embodied more selfless devotion than did the eminent King. If our devotion makes us proud, or is performed to be recognized and approved by others, then it ceases to be for God. It serves the self rather than being the path to transcendence. The inner sincerity of the devotee makes an act devotional, not its religious context. Only this sincerity connects the devotee to the Divine Beloved.

Look, you brothers,
who bathe in the holy waters,
Look, you monks,
who bathe in the stream.
Give up, give up,
your unholy thoughts;
Give up lustful thoughts
for another man's wife,
Give up coveting
after another man's wealth.
If you bathe in the waters
without giving up these,
It is as if bathing in a stream
that has run dry.

HINDUISM: BASAVANNA, VACANA 642

What is Shinto?
Not in the shrines
the worldly minded
frequent for gifts
in vain, but in good deeds,
pure of heart,
lies real religion.

SHINTO: GENCHI KATO

When King David had completed the Book of
Psalms, he felt exceedingly proud, and said:
"Lord of the Universe, is there a creature that
proclaims more praises of You than I?"
God thereupon sent to him a frog, which said:
"David, take not such pride in yourself. I chant
the praises of my Creator more than you do.
Moreover, I am performing a great Mitzvah. For
when my time to expire is at hand, I go to the
shore of the sea, and permit myself to be
swallowed up by one of its creatures. Thus even
my death is a deed of kindness."

JUDAISM: YALKUT SHIMEONI, II, 889.

Make your mosque of compassion,
your prayer mat of sincerity;
Your Qur'an of honest and legitimate earning.
Be modesty your circumcision,
noble conduct your Ramadan fast –
Thus shall you be a true Muslim.
Make good deeds your Kaaba;
truth your preceptor;
Good action your creed and daily prayers.
Make your rosary of what pleases God:
Thus will you be honored at the last reckoning.

SIKHISM: ADI GRANTH, VAR MAJH, M.L, P.140

Finite and transient are the fruits of sacrificial rites. The deluded, who regard them as the highest good, remain subject to birth and death. Attached to works, they know not God. Works lead them only to heaven, whence, to their sorrow, their rewards quickly exhausted, they are flung back to earth.

Considering religion to be observance of rituals and performance of acts of charity, the deluded remain ignorant of the highest good. Having enjoyed in heaven the reward of their good works, they enter again into the world of mortals. But wise, self-controlled, and tranquil souls, who are contented in spirit, and who practice austerity and meditation in solitude and silence, are freed from all impurity, and attain by the path of liberation to the immortal, the truly existing, the changeless Self.

HINDUISM: MUNDAKA UPANISHAD 1.2.7–11

RIGHT
Portrait of a man reading, Khurasan, c. 1575-80.

Krishna said to Arjuna, "It is extremely difficult to obtain the vision you have had; even the gods long to see me in this aspect. Neither knowledge of the scriptures, nor austerities, nor charity, nor sacrifice can bring the vision you have seen. But through unfailing devotion, Arjuna, you can know me, see me, and attain union with me. Whoever makes me the supreme goal of all his works and acts without selfish attachments, who devotes himself to me completely and is free from ill will for any creature, enters into me."

HINDUISM: BHAGAVAD GITA CH.11

With what shall I come before the Lord and bow myself before God on high? Shall I come before him with burnt offerings, with calves a year old? Will the Lord be pleased with thousands of rams, with ten thousand rivers of oil? Shall I give my firstborn for my transgression, the fruit of my body for the sin of my soul?

He has showed you, O man, what is good; and what does the Lord require of you but to do justice, and to love kindness, and to walk humbly with your God?

JUDAISM AND CHRISTIANITY: MICAH 6.6–8

CHAPTER EIGHT

Fate and Free Will

MOST SCRIPTURES TEACH us that we have moral freedom and should choose to act well. Many, however, also teach that God is all powerful and predestines everything by divine will. Every religion wrestles to make sense of this profound paradox.

Some scriptures suggest that while the external conditions which we encounter in our lives are preordained by God, our internal reactions to them are not. Human life is the interaction of fate and freedom of choice. We cannot control the world, but we can control our responses to it. In the face of such knowledge, spiritual seekers should cultivate an equanimous acceptance of all that God decrees. If God is creating their fate they can live without anxiety and fear, for everything is safely in the divine hands.

Free will is often seen as both the problem and the solution. We suffer because of our selfish desires and actions, which do not coincide with God's will. The spiritual use of free will is to freely give it up – to surrender the personal will to the will of God. Certain scriptures, however, see even this act of surrender as possible only by God's grace. Everything is an act of God, including our thoughts and actions. This sublime truth is obscured by the personal self which mistakenly believes that it is the "doer" and the "thinker." In reality, all is one and there is no independent personal self to be free or otherwise.

These arguments are really different perspectives on the same truth. From the perspective of the Oneness of God, there is no free will, because everything is the unfolding of one thing. From the point of view of the separateness experienced by unenlightened human beings, there is freedom of choice, because everything is the interaction of separate things. How can both be true? This is a mystical paradox which cannot be solved by the rational mind, but only dissolved in the experience of enlightenment.

OPPOSITE
Symbol of Matthew,
"Imago Hominus,"
Lindisfarne, c. 700.

FATE

Scripture teaches that God is all-powerful and decrees the fate appropriate for each individual. According to Jewish scripture, even the insignificant details of our lives, such as bruising a finger, are decreed by heaven. The Chinese sage Mencius accepts the failure of a prince to visit him as an act of heaven, not the machinations of a conniving courtier. Something impels us to do all that we do, and it is therefore ridiculous to talk of responsibility. Islamic scripture sees fate as so binding that a man could be on the threshold of heaven, yet his destiny could suddenly lead him to begin performing evil acts. Likewise a man on the threshold of hell could be fated to change his ways suddenly and end up in paradise.

The Talmud describes an unborn soul being shown the fate which awaits it. Whatever fortunes or misfortunes lie ahead, every soul has the capacity to learn the law. Unlike the Muslim Hadith, Jewish scripture here suggests that one thing alone is not predestined – whether the person will be good or bad. This is the domain of personal free will.

Where you fall, there your God pushed you down.
God has both the yam and the knife; only those whom he gives a slice can eat!

INDIGENOUS RELIGIONS: IGBO PROVERBS
FROM NIGERIA

Yueh-cheng Tzu saw Mencius. "I mentioned you to the prince," said he, "and he was to have come to see you. Among his favorites is one Tsang Ts'ang who dissuaded him. That is why he failed to come."

"When a man goes forward," said Mencius, "there is something which urges him on; when he halts, there is something which holds him back. It is not in his power either to go forward or to halt. It is due to Heaven that I failed to meet the Marquis of Lu. How can this fellow Tsang be responsible for my failure?"

CONFUCIANISM: MENCIUS I.B.16

No man bruises his finger here on earth unless it was so decreed against him in Heaven.

JUDAISM: HULLIN 7B

For not of your will were you formed, and not of your own will were you born, and not of your will do you live, and not of your own will will you die.

JUDAISM: ABOT 4.29

RIGHT
Christ at the Marriage Feast at Cana, *Paolo Veronese (1528-88).*

Before the soul is given residence in the body of a child about to he born, the kernel of the body is brought to the Heavenly Tribunal, where it receives its fate: whether the child will enjoy riches or poverty; whether it be male or female, heroic or cowardly, tall or short, handsome or homely, fat or thin, respected or ignored. One thing, however, is not subjected to predestination, namely whether the child will be good or bad, since it must have freedom of will.

A soul is given residence despite any protestations in the body to be born. It is then given over to an angel who endows it with the capacity of learning the whole Torah and of performing all the Mitzwot. It is taken to Paradise, and the angel says: "These were souls in bodies like yours, and because they did well in life, they are now enjoying their reward." Next it is taken to Gehenna, and the angel declares: "These were like you, and they did evil. Do not imitate them." Then the soul is returned to the womb.

JUDAISM: TANHUMA TO TAZRIA

Nothing will happen to us except what God has decreed for us: He is our Protector.

ISLAM: QUR'AN 9.51

It may be that one of you will be performing the works of the people of Paradise, so that between him and Paradise there is the distance of only an arm's length, but then what is written for him overtakes him, and he begins to perform the works of the people of hell, into which he will go.

Or maybe one of you will be performing the works of the people of hell, so that between him and hell there is the distance of only an arm's length, but then what is written for him will overtake him, and he will begin to perform the works of the people of Paradise, into which he will go.

ISLAM: FORTY HADITH OF AN-NAWAWI 4

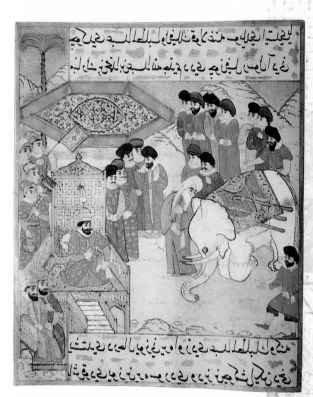

SURRENDER TO GOD

Scripture teaches that we are in God's divine care and need have no fear. We should surrender our personal anxieties and desires and have complete trust in God to give us all we need in life. Those who live in fear do not have faith in God's will for them. If we trust our fate, however, we can surrender our worry and trepidation.

In the Gospel of Matthew, Jesus considers how God cares for even the lilies in the fields. They do not need to work for their livelihood, yet are more splendid that the great King Solomon. If God provides even for the flowers, we too can be confident of his paternal care. If we first seek goodness, rather than material security, then all we need will come to us by God's grace. In a similar spirit, Confucius points out that nature is not burdened with anxiety for the future. It does not think about things, but spontaneously returns to the Source. We should do likewise.

Any who believes in his Lord has no fear, either of loss or of any injustice.

ISLAM: QUR'AN 72.13

If God is for us, who can be against us?

CHRISTIANITY: ROMANS 8.31

BELOW
Illumination for the Sermon on the Mount, English, c. 1870.

Don't be anxious about your life; what you'll have to eat and drink, or what you will wear to cover your body. Life is more than food, and the body is more than clothing. Look at the birds in the air. They don't sow or reap or harvest, and yet your Heavenly Father feeds them. Aren't you more valuable to him than the birds?
Who can add anything to his lifespan through being anxious? Why are you worried about clothing? Look at the lilies in the fields. They just grow, without needing to work or spin, yet even Solomon in all his glory was not so splendid. If God clothes the fields so magnificently, will he not clothe you? O men of little faith! Don't be anxious, saying, "What shall we eat?" or "What shall we wear?" Your heavenly Father knows what you need. First seek his kingdom and his goodness, and all these things shall be yours as well.

CHRISTIANITY: MATTHEW 6.25–33

*Whoever has bread in his basket
and says, "What am I going to eat
tomorrow?" only belongs to those
who are little in faith.*

JUDAISM: SOTA 48B

*If God gives you a cup of wine and
an evil-minded person kicks it over,
He fills it up for you again.*

INDIGENOUS RELIGIONS: AKAN PROVERB
FROM GHANA

*The Master said, "What need has
nature of thought and care? In
nature all things return to their
common Source and are distributed
along different paths; through one
action, the fruits of a hundred
thoughts are realized. What need has
nature of thought, of care?"*

CONFUCIANISM: I CHING, GREAT
COMMENTARY 2.5.1

*My Lord is boundless
as the sun and moon,
Lighting heaven and earth;
How then can I have concerns
about what is to be?*

SHINTO: MAN'YOSHU 20

RIGHT
*Illumination from a
manuscript of
St. Matthew's
Gospel, Chapter V,
English, c. 1870.*

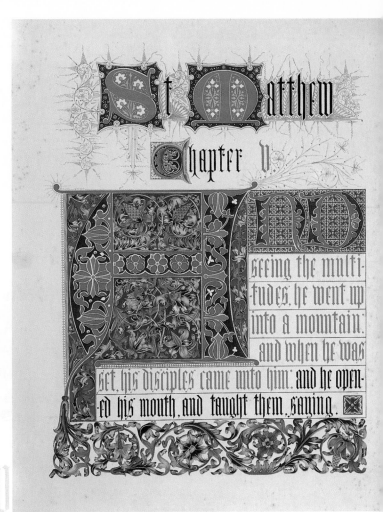

WE ARE WHERE GOD WANTS US

God has placed us exactly where he wants us, and scripture recommends that we humbly accept our position. It is better to be content with what we are, than to envy others. Jewish scripture teaches that social differences are of no importance, provided that we direct our hearts to heaven. Confucius describes the moral person as someone who finds the way to live a virtuous life in any situation. They calmly await the fate that God has preordained for them.

Scripture is not advocating resignation or apathetic acceptance of social injustice. If we feel the need to transform our present situation, that need and any actions which may result from it are also part of our fate. Acceptance is not passive abdication of involvement with life. It is actively engaging with things as they are, rather than getting lost in how we would like them to be. Adopting either an attitude of fighting life or putting up with life causes us to suffer. Acceptance is about transmuting these judgmental attitudes into fully embracing life as it is.

BELOW
Adoration of the Magi, and the marriage feast at Cana, from Liber Sacramentorum Fulda, *German.*

Borrowed trousers and garments
Never fit a man well;
They are usually either too tight,
Or too loose.
Proper fitting is achieved
When one wears one's own dress.

INDIGENOUS RELIGIONS: YORUBA PROVERB
FROM NIGERIA

A favorite saying of the rabbis of Jabneh was, I am God's creature and my peasant neighbor is God's creature. My work is in the town and his work is in the country. I rise early for my work and he rises early for his work. Just as he does not presume to do my work, so I do not presume to do his work. Will you say, I do much and he does little? We have learned, one may do much or one may do little; it is all the same, provided he directs his heart to Heaven.

JUDAISM: BERAKOT 17A

All appointments are from Heaven, even that of a janitor.

JUDAISM: BABA BATRA 91B

*T*he moral man conforms himself to his life circumstances; he does not desire anything outside his position. Finding himself in a position of wealth and honor, he lives as becomes one living in a position of wealth and honor. Finding himself in a position of poverty and humble circumstances, he lives as becomes one living in a position of poverty and humble circumstances. Finding himself in uncivilized countries, he lives as becomes one living in uncivilized countries. Finding himself in circumstances of danger and difficulty, he acts according to what is required of a man under such circumstances. In one word, the moral man can find himself in no situation in life in which he is not master of himself.

In high position he does not domineer over his subordinates. In a subordinate position he does not court the favors of his superiors. He puts in order his own personal conduct and seeks nothing from others; hence he has no complaint to make. He complains not against God, nor rails against men.

Thus it is that the moral man lives out the even tenor of his life, calmly waiting for the appointment of God, whereas the vulgar person takes to dangerous courses, expecting the uncertain chances of luck.

CONFUCIANISM: DOCTRINE OF THE MEAN 14

RIGHT
The kiss of Judas and Jesus before Pilate, Psalter of Ingeburg of Denmark, *French, 13th century.*

ACCEPTANCE OF MISFORTUNE

God is the source of our fortunes and misfortunes, and scripture teaches that both should be accepted with equanimity. Jain scripture advises a monk to be content with uncertainty. In the Ad Granath, Guru Nanak reflects to himself that it is futile to ask for pleasure when suffering comes, for both are robes that must be worn. A true lover is forever absorbed in the Beloved, whether the lover is treated well or badly.

In Jewish scripture God tests the faith of his servant Job by allowing Satan to curse him with terrible afflictions. Despite his wife's incredulity, Job maintains that it is foolish to expect to receive only good from God's hand. In times of adversity, Ecclesiastes teaches us to consider that the same God also gave us our times of prosperity. There is natural rhythm to life and a time for all things. Understanding and accepting this, the wise live in harmony with life's changing seasons, knowing that good will inevitably follow bad, as spring the winter. To wish for only prosperity is as unnatural as demanding a perpetual summer.

It is not only physical bravery that counts. One must have the courage to face life as it is, to go through sorrows, and always sacrifice oneself for the sake of others.

INDIGENOUS RELIGIONS: KIPSIGIS SAYING
FROM KENYA

"My clothes are torn, I shall soon go naked," or "I shall get a new suit:" such thoughts should not be entertained by a monk. At one time he will have no clothes, at another time he will have some. Knowing this to be a salutary rule, a wise monk should not complain about it.

JAINISM: UTTARADHYAYANA SUTRA 2.12–13

Nanak, for man it is idle to ask for pleasure when suffering comes; Pleasure and suffering are like robes which man must wear as they come. Where arguing is of no avail, it is best to be contented.

SIKHISM. ADI GRANTH, VAR MAJH M.1

What kind of love is this that to another can shift? Says Nanak, True lovers are those who are forever absorbed in the Beloved. Whoever discriminates between treatment held good or bad, is not a true lover – he rather is caught in calculations.

SIKHISM. ADI GRANTH, ASA-KI-VAR M.2

Satan went forth from the presence of the Lord, and afflicted Job with loathsome sores from the sole of his foot to the crown of his head. And he took a piece of broken pottery with which to scrape himself, and sat among the ashes. Then his wife said to him, "Do you still hold fast to your integrity? Curse God, and die." But he said to her, "You speak as one of the foolish women would speak. Shall we receive good at the hand of God, and shall we not receive evil?"

JUDAISM AND CHRISTIANITY: JOB 2.7–10

In the day of prosperity be joyful, and in the day of adversity consider; God made the one as well as the other, so that man may never know what will come to be.

JUDAISM AND CHRISTIANITY: ECCLESIASTES

7–14

For everything there is a season, and a time for every matter under heaven: a time to be born, and a time to die; a time to plant, and a time to pluck up what is planted; a time to kill, and a time to heal; a time to break down, and a time to build up; a time to weep, and a time to laugh; a time to mourn, and a time to dance; a time to cast away stones, and a time to gather stones together; a time to embrace, and a time to refrain from embracing; a time to seek, and a time to lose; a time to keep, and a time to cast away; a time to rend, and a time to sew; a time to keep silence, and a time to speak; a time to love, and a time to hate; a time for war, and a time for peace.

JUDAISM AND CHRISTIANITY: ECCLESIASTES

3.1–8

LEFT
Job being tested by God, from a medieval manuscript.

EPICTETUS ON CONTROL

The ancient Stoic sage Epictetus teaches that happiness and freedom lie in understanding a basic principle: some things are within our control and others are not. If we try to change what we cannot change, we will live a frustrated life. If we fail to take responsibility for what we can change, we will lose our true freedom. The external world is largely beyond our control and should be accepted as it is. The internal world of our aspirations and opinions is within our control, however. We cannot control the external world, but we can control our responses to it. We are free to adopt a positive, accepting attitude. Such an attitude is the key to happiness.

Happiness and freedom begin with a clear understanding of one principle: some things are within our control, and some things are not. It is only after you have faced up to this fundamental rule and learned to distinguish between what you can and can't control that inner tranquility and outer effectiveness become possible.

Within our control are our own opinions, aspirations, desires, and the things that repel us. These areas are quite rightly our concern, because they are directly subject to our influence. We always have a choice about the contents and character of our inner lives.

Outside our control, however, are such things as what kind of body we have, whether we're born into wealth or strike it rich, how we are regarded by others, and our status in society. We must remember that those things are externals and are therefore not our concern. Trying to control or to change what we can't only results in torment.

Remember: the things within our power are naturally at our disposal, free from any restraint or hindrance; but those things outside our power are weak, dependent, or determined by whims and actions of others. Remember, too, that if you think that you have free rein over things that are naturally beyond your control or if you attempt to adopt the affairs of others as your own, your pursuits will be thwarted and you will become a frustrated, anxious, and faultfinding person.

ANCIENT MYSTERY RELIGIONS: EPICTETUS

RIGHT
The procession of St. Gregory, Soane Book of Hours.

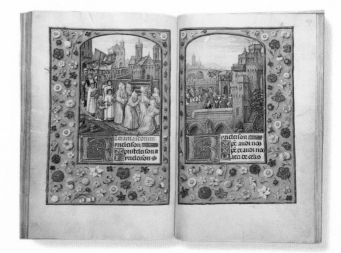

KARMA

Hindu and Buddhist scriptures explain the relationship between fate and free will by the law of karma. Karma is a form of cosmic justice by which our present actions bring about our future fate. If we harm others, we will be harmed ourselves. If we act well, good things will come to us. Our present fate is a product of free choices in the past. Our free reactions to our present fate will create our future. Sometimes karma is seen as taking a long time to manifest. Like seeds that slowly ripen, the results of our actions may take years or even lifetimes to return to us.

This philosophy of fate as a sort of cosmic justice which rewards and punishes our free actions is found in various forms in all traditions. At its heart is the simple idea that we reap the harvest of the seeds that we sow. If we sow selfishness, we will reap suffering. If we sow selflessness, we will reap liberation.

If for my own sake,
I cause harm to others,
I shall be tormented in hellish realms;
But if for the sake of others
I cause harm to myself,
I shall acquire all that is magnificent.
By holding myself in high esteem
I shall find myself in unpleasant
realms, ugly and stupid;
But should this attitude
be shifted to others
I shall acquire honors
in a joyful realm.
If I employ others
for my own purposes
I myself shall experience servitude,
But if I use myself
for the sake of others
I shall experience only lordliness.

BUDDHISM: SHANTIDEVA, GUIDE TO THE
BODHISATTVA'S WAY OF LIFE 8.126–28

Whatever affliction may visit you is
for what your own hands have
earned.

ISLAM: QUR'AN 42.30

As sweet as honey is an evil deed, so
thinks the fool so long as it ripens not;
but when it ripens, then he comes to
grief.
An evil deed committed does not
immediately bear fruit, just as milk
does not curdle at once; but like a
smoldering fire covered with ashes, it
remains with the fool until the
moment it ignites and burns him.

BUDDHISM: DHAMMAPADA 69,71

Do not be deceived; God is not
mocked, for whatever a man sows,
that he will also reap.

CHRISTIANITY: GALATIANS 6.7

Those who wrongfully kill men are
only putting their weapons into the
hands of others who will in turn kill
them.

TAOISM: TREATISE ON RESPONSE AND
RETRIBUTION 5

GOD DOES EVERYTHING

Some scriptures teach that as there is in reality only the Oneness of God, God does everything. When we think we act, it is actually God who is acting through us. When we think we think, it is actually God who is thinking through us. God is the Oneness that operates through the multiplicity of which we are a part.

The Sufi master Rumi compares us to a bowl floating on water. The bowl moves, but only because the water moves. In the same way, God not humankind is the author of all actions. Most people are merely unconscious agents of God's will. Someone who is aware that he is God's vehicle is truly great. Sikh scripture says that the Lord is the doer and cause of all. Not even enlightenment is due to human efforts for everything happens only by the will of God.

The Bhagavad Gita states that only the deluded think of themselves as the doer. The illumined know that everything is happening through the natural interaction of the different *gunas* or "qualities" of the universe. The Ashtavakra Gita describes the individual who is identified with his separate self as mistakenly believing that he is the doer. An enlightened being, without this sense of being a personal self, knows he does not act, even though he seems to do so. He is without a will of his own and therefore accepts with equanimity whatever arises naturally in his life. He is simply part of the oneness.

In the Jewish Ode of Solomon, the writer compares himself to a harp which is played by God. The recently discovered Dead Sea Scrolls include a great hymn to God's omnipotence. Nothing can be done, except by God. If we think we speak, it is actually God who has opened our mouth. There is nothing besides God. God does all, because God is all. There is no separate human self independent of the Oneness of God, so there is ultimately no one to be free or otherwise.

BELOW
The Crucifixion, *by the Boucicault master.*

*Should you do anything that is beautiful, God has caused it to be beautiful.
Should you do anything evil, God has caused it to be evil.*

INDIGENOUS RELIGIONS:

NUPE PROVERB FROM

NIGERIA

*The Lord is the Doer, cause of all:
What avail man's designs?
As is the Lord's will, so it happens.
The Lord is Almighty, without impediment to His will.
All that is done is by His pleasure:
He is One and All.*

SIKHISM: ADI GRANTH,

GAURI SUKHMANI, M.5

We are like a bowl on the surface of the water. The movement of the bowl on the surface of the water is controlled not by the bowl but by the water. Hence we realize absolutely that the creator of man's acts is not man but God.

Man is like a bow in the hand of the grip of God's omnipotence. God most High employs him upon various tasks, and the agent in reality is God, not the bow. The bow is the instrument and the medium, but it is unaware and unconscious of God, that the world's order may be maintained. Mighty indeed is the bow that is aware in whose hand it is!

ISLAM: DISCOURSES OF RUMI 41 AND 54

All actions are performed by the gunas of prakriti. Deluded by his identification with the ego, a person thinks, "I am the doer." But the illumined man or woman understands the domain of the gunas and is not attached. Such people know that the gunas interact with each other; they do not claim to be the doer.

HINDUISM: BHAGAVAD GITA CHAPTER 3

Worldly men are convinced of the idea "I am the agent," and bound by the idea "another is the agent." They don't truly understand. They have not seen it as a thorn. For one who looks at this thorn with caution, the ideas "I am the agent" and "another is the agent" do not exist.

BUDDHISM: UDANA 70

Neither utterance nor silence lies within man's power; Neither to ask nor to give. Neither life nor death depends on man's effort. Authority, wealth, or command – none of these come by man's own endeavor; Nor meditation, enlightenment, or cogitation. Not by his own effort and spiritual practice Will a man escape free of worldliness. God alone has the power and exercises it.

SIKHISM: ADI GRANTH, JAPUJI 33, M.L

BELOW
Abu-Zayd preaching in the Mosque of Samarkand, from "The Maqamat."

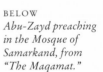

*Why should the serene one who is
aware of the emptiness of all
phenomenal objects have any
preferences for things as being
acceptable or unacceptable.
He who has ceased to conceptualize
and is, therefore, free from
attachment to sense objects, beyond
the interrelated pairs of opposites, and
free from volition, accepts with
equanimity whatever comes his way
in the normal course.
The identified individual with a
sense of volition acts even if he is not
acting. On the other hand, the
enlightened being, without any sense
of personal doership, does not act
even if there is action.*

HINDUISM: ASHTAVAKRA GITA 58, 59,
AND 205

*As the hand moves over the harp
and the strings speak
so the spirit of the Lord speaks
in my members
and I speak by his love,*

JUDAISM: ODES OF SOLOMON 6

*What is man, mere earth,
kneaded out of clay,
destined to return to the dust,
that You should give him insight
into such wonders
and make him privy to things divine?
As for me,
I am but dust and ashes.
What can I devise
except You have desired it?
And what can I think
apart from Your will?
And how be strong
except You have stayed me,
or use my mind except
You have created it?
How speak
except You have opened my mouth?
How reply
except You have given me sense?
You are the Prince of the angels,
and the King of all that are in glory,
and the Lord of every spirit,
and the Ruler of every deed.
Without You nothing is done,
and without Your will
can nothing be known.
None there is beside You,
and none to share Your power
and none to match Your glory,
and Your power is beyond price.
Which among all Your great
wondrous works
has power to stand before You?
How much less, then,
can he who returns to dust
attain to such power.
Only for Your own glory
have You done all these things.*

JUDAISM: DEAD SEA SCROLLS

RIGHT
*Detail from
the procession
of St. Gregory,*
Soane Book
of Hours.

THE PARADOX

Scripture presents us with a mysterious paradox. On the one hand we are exhorted to choose to live a good life. On the other we are told that God is the one doer of all actions, which leaves no room for human free will. Jewish scripture boldly states this paradox as a mystical truth. It also suggests that fate and human will mysteriously coincide, that life leads us along the road that we have actually chosen.

Jain scripture sees it as a miracle that no one blames the great teacher Mahavira for the inherent contradictions in his teachings. It also addresses the problem of the origination of karma. Karma attempts to resolve the contradiction between fate and free will by explaining fate as a product of our previous choices. But if our present destiny is a product of our past actions, how did karma arise before there were any past actions? The Jain answer is to accept the paradox and see the relationship between the soul and karma as beginningless.

The paradoxes produced by trying to understanding the mysteries of fate and free will are inherent in any attempt to conceive of an ultimate unity. Any concept is inevitably caught in the duality that characterizes all thought. Mystical paradoxes cannot be understood rationally, because with them we reach the frontier of thinking. They ask us to step out into an intuitive spiritual understanding which can embrace opposite poles. Objectively all is one, and we are puppets of fate. Subjectively the world is made up of individual separate things, and we experience freedom of choice. The highest spiritual understanding is to embrace these seemingly contradictory statements as equally true, because although separateness may be an illusion, the fact that we experience this illusion is itself part of the oneness.

The irony is that when we experience ourselves as separate individuals with personal freedom of choice, we also experience being trapped in a world which we cannot control. But when we embrace having no personal free will and know the Oneness of God, we are liberated to become Pure Consciousness witnessing the unfolding processes of a life that can never harm us. The experience of free will actually imprisons us, and the acceptance of fate sets us free.

*Everything is foreknown,
but man is free.*

JUDAISM: MISHNAH, ABOT 3.19

It can be proved by the Torah, the Prophets and the other sacred writings, that man is led along the road which he wishes to follow.

JUDAISM: MAKKOT 10B

My feet lead me to the place I love.

JUDAISM: SUKKAH 53

The question as to when the union of soul with karma occurred for the first time cannot arise, since this is a beginningless relation like gold and stone.

JAINISM: PANCADHYAYI 2.35–36

Lord Mahavira! Your word sometimes supports the view of providence, at other times calls events spontaneously occurring or ascribes destiny to external factors. At times you hold the deeds of individuals to be the mold of their desert, at other times find that another's deeds project their moral reflection on the individual. The miracle is that none blames you for these paradoxical utterances!

JAINISM: SIDDHASENA, DVATRIMSHIKA 3.8

LEFT
*The Annunciation,
from* The Hastings
Hours.

CHAPTER NINE

Death

ONE OF THE MOST PROFOUND mysteries of life is that it ends in death. Helping us understand this unavoidable fact is one of the major functions of religion. From a materialist perspective, death is extinction. Spiritual traditions give us a more optimistic view. Death is seen only as the annihilation of the body. The soul survives in an afterlife. In some traditions the soul reincarnates into another human body. Death is often viewed as a moment of judgment of all that we have been in life. This judgment decides the fate of the soul after death, whether it will experience a purifying purgatorial existence or a satisfying heavenly existence. Our condition in the afterlife is dependent on our present life.

Scripture urges us not to avert our eyes from the inevitable end, but to live with an awareness of death. Death is not a meaningless tragedy, but actually gives meaning to life. Dwelling on death helps us realize the value of life. It enables us to see clearly what is important and what is trivial. Spirituality teaches us not to become preoccupied with the transitory things of life that we must leave behind us at death, but rather to develop those qualities that will continue to benefit us in the life hereafter.

Ultimately, the duality of life and death can be transcended in a vision of the Oneness of God. We do not need to wait for death to experience this. By dying to the separate self while alive the enlightened sage sees beyond all opposites, including life and death, and knows that which is immortal and permanent. The Zen masters teach "while alive be a dead man." The Sufis say "die before death." St. Paul writes "I die daily." The ancient philosopher Socrates says that all of philosophy is a meditation on death. For a man who has already "died," death holds no fear and life no attraction. He knows himself to be pure consciousness – the eternal witness of all.

OPPOSITE
Original bark painting of a funeral ceremony on Croker Island, Australian.

CONTEMPLATING DEATH

Death is often seen as an unpleasant subject that is best avoided. Scripture, however, recommends that we face our mortality. The Muslim Hadith teaches us to live with the awareness that death could visit us at any time. The Hindu Institutes of Vishnu point out the unavoidable nature of death which comes inevitably when the karma from a soul's previous existence is exhausted. The Buddhist Majjhima Nikaya advises monks to spend time with dead bodies and to contemplate that the same fate will befall their bodies.

By living with death, the spiritual seeker does not delude himself into a false sense of permanence. The moment and manner of death may be unknown, but that it will happen is certain. Spirituality teaches us to prepare for this eventuality as the fulfillment of life, to become conscious while healthy of the corruptible body that we inhabit, so that when illness and death comes, it is not a complete shock nor a profound spiritual challenge. Dwelling on death is not macabre. It can lessen our identification with the mortal body and awaken an intuitive knowledge of the immortal soul. Through facing the fear of death, this fear can be overcome.

BELOW
A Japanese funeral, 19th century.

In the evening do not expect to live till morning, and in the morning do not expect evening. Prepare as long as you are in good health for sickness, and so long as you are alive for death.

ISLAM: FORTY HADITH OF AN-NAWAWI 40

Remember, those who fear death shall not escape it, and those who aspire to immortality shall not achieve it.

ISLAM: NAHJUL BALAGHA, SERMON 43

Be of an exceedingly humble spirit, for the end of man is the worm.

JUDAISM: ABOT 4.4

Time is no one's friend and no one's enemy; when the effect of his acts in a former existence, by which his present existence is caused, has expired, time snatches a man away forcibly. A man will not die before his time has come, even though he has been pierced by a thousand shafts; he will not live after his time is out, even though he has only been touched by the point of a blade of grass. Neither drugs, nor magical formulas, nor burnt offerings, nor prayers will save a man who is in the bonds of death or old age. An impending evil cannot be averted even by a hundred precautions; what reason then for you to complain?

HINDUISM: INSTITUTES OF VISHNU 20.43–46

Tzu Lu asked about worship of ghosts and spirits. Confucius said: "We don't yet know how to serve men, how can we know about serving the spirits?" "What about death?" was the next question. Confucius said: "We don't yet know about life, how can we know about death?"

CONFUCIANISM: ANALECTS XI, 11

What awaits men at death they do not expect or even imagine.

ANCIENT MYSTERY RELIGIONS: HERACLITUS

LXXXIV

A rabbit that a huntsman brings,
They pay for it the proper price;
But none will give a betel nut
For the corpse of a ruler of the land!
A man's body is less worth than a rabbit's.

HINDUISM: BASAVANNA, VACANA 158

LEFT
The death of Buddha, his cremation and the division of his remains, from the Parinirvana, Tibetan, 18th century.

A monk reflects on this very body enveloped by the skin and full of manifold impurity from the soles up and from the crown of the head down, thinking, "There are in this body: hair of the head, hair of the body, nails, teeth, skin, flesh, sinews, bones, marrow, kidney, heart, liver, membranes, spleen, lungs, bowels, intestines, faeces, bile, phlegm, pus, blood, sweat, fat, saliva, mucus, urine."
And further, if a monk sees a body dead that is one, two or three days old, swollen, discolored, decomposing, thrown aside in the cemetery, he applies this perception to his own body, "Truly, this body of mine, too, is of the same nature, it will become like that and will not escape it."

BUDDHISM: MAJJHIMA NIKAYA I.55–63,
SATIPATTHANA SUTTA

DEATH AND LIFE

Scripture teaches that we are are only temporary visitors to this world and should use our lives to prepare for what awaits us in death. In the New Testament, Jesus advises us to lay up our treasures in heaven, not here on earth where we will inevitably lose them. The Adi Granath recommends that we be shrewd business people who trade only in commodities which will accompany us after death. What can we take with us? Obviously nothing which exists in the outer objective world of things. What we are – our inner qualities – is all that will accompany us. Spiritual wealth is a better long-term investment than the largest material fortune.

Tenrikyo states that our bodies are only on loan from God, and we should ask ourselves how we are using them. Confucius sees the key to facing death contentedly as first knowing the Tao. For Chuang Tzu, death is not to be anticipated with fear. For him, life is an illness and death is the cure.

BELOW
Fighting at the gates of Jerusalem; the burial of Muhammad, Turkish, 1583.

This world is like a vestibule before the World to Come; prepare yourself in the vestibule that you may enter the hall.
Happy is the man who in his hour of death is as pure as he was in his hour of birth.

JUDAISM: ABOT 4.21 AND Y. MEGILLAH 1, 9

Don't store up your treasure on earth, where moths and rust consume it and thieves break in and steal it. But store your treasure in heaven, where moths and rust can't consume it and thieves can't break in and steal it. For where your treasure is, there will your heart be also.

CHRISTIANITY: MATTHEW 6.19–21

All are afraid of death; nowhere is there fearlessness. But the virtuous saints never fear death and the state after death.

HINDUISM: MATSYA PURANA 212.25

O shrewd businessman, do only profitable business:
Deal only in that commodity which shall accompany you after death.

SIKHISM: ADI GRANTH, SRI RAGA M. 1

All human bodies are things lent by God. With what thought are you using yours?

SHINTO: TENRIKYO. OFUDESAKI 3.41

Confucius said, "Having heard the Way (Tao) in the morning, one may die content in the evening."

CONFUCIANISM: ANALECTS IV 8

Look upon life as a swelling tumor, a protruding goiter, and upon death as the draining of a sore or the bursting of a boil.

TAOISM: CHUANG TZU 6

A PERSONAL JOURNEY

The Buddhist Guide to the Bodhisattva's Way of Life warns us that death will not wait for us to be ready. When it comes, all the evils that we have done will be seen to have been pointless, and all of the pleasures like fleeting dreams. Although friends and foes have passed away, however, the evil actions we have performed on their behalf have sowed the karmic seeds of what lies ahead for us. Death is a radical reappraisal of what we have done and what we have been. It is a journey that we have to face alone. Although we may be surrounded by our loved ones on our deathbed, they will not be able to help us. Only spiritual understanding, which in life we may have tragically ignored, will see us through the experience of death.

Single is each being born; single it dies; single it enjoys the reward of its virtue; single it suffers the punishment of its sin.

HINDUISM: LAWS OF MANU 4.240

*The untrustworthy lord of death
waits not for things to be done
or undone;
Whether I am sick or healthy,
this fleeting life span is unstable.
Leaving all I must depart alone.
Through not having understood this
I committed various kinds of evil
for the sake of my friends and foes.
Yet my foes will become nothing.
My friends will become nothing.
I too will become nothing.
Likewise all will become nothing.
Just like a dream experience,
whatever things I enjoy
will become a memory.*

*Whatever has passed
will not be seen again.
Even within this brief life
many friends and foes have passed,
but whatever unbearable evil
I committed for them
remains ahead of me.
While I am lying in bed,
although surrounded by my friends
and relatives,
the feeling of life being severed
will be experienced by me alone.
When seized
by the messengers of death,
what benefit will friends
and relatives afford?
My merit alone shall protect me then,
but upon that I have never relied.*

BUDDHISM: SHANTIDEVA, GUIDE TO THE
BODHISATTVA'S WAY OF LIFE 2.33–41

GRIEF

The death of a loved one is usually accompanied by the powerful experience of grief. A valued physical presence with which we have become familiar is suddenly and finally removed, and we are engulfed by a sense of the impermanence of everything. This Nahuatl Lament beautifully conveys the poignancy of such loss and the desperate need to find a way to connect with the departed.

Grief awakens us to the transitory nature of life and can propel us into a deep intuitive understanding of the love which transcends death. Chuang Tzu expresses such an understanding. He is undisturbed by the death of his wife because he understands the natural and inevitable changes that we all must undergo and faces death with acceptance and confidence.

Weeping, I, the singer, weave my song of flowers of sadness; I call to memory the youths, the shards, the fragments, gone to the land of the dead; once noble and powerful here on earth, the youths were dried up like feathers, were split into fragments like an emerald, before the face and in the sight of those who saw them on earth, and with the knowledge of the Cause of All.

Alas! Alas! I sing in grief as I recall the children. Would that I could turn back again; would that I could grasp their hands once more; would that I could call them forth from the land of the dead; would that we could bring them again on earth, that they might rejoice and delight the Giver of Life; is it possible that we His servants

should reject him or should be ungrateful? Thus I weep in my heart as I, the singer, review my memories, recalling things sad and grievous.

Would only that I knew they could hear me, there in the land of the dead, were I to sing some worthy song. Would that I could gladden them, that I could console the suffering and the torment of the children. How can it be learned? Whence can I draw the inspiration? They are not where I may follow them; neither can I reach them with my calling as one here on earth.

INDIGENOUS RELIGIONS: A NAHUATL
LAMENT FROM MEXICO

RIGHT
The Deposition of Christ, *Di Bondone Giotto (1276-1337).*

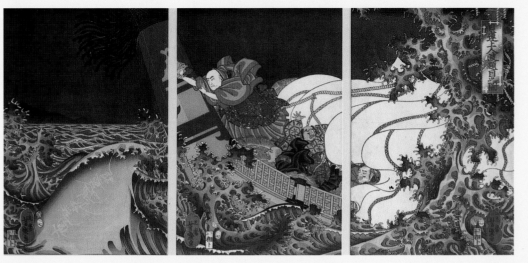

LEFT
*Nichiren calming
the storm with an
invocation by
Yoshimoro,
Japanese, 1857.*

Chuang Tzu's wife died. When Hui Tzu went to convey his condolences, he found Chuang Tzu sitting with his legs sprawled out, pounding on a tub and singing. "You lived with her, she brought up your children and grew old." Said Hui Tzu, "It should be enough simply not to weep at her death. But pounding on a tub and singing – this is going too far, isn't it?"

Chuang Tzu said, "You're wrong. When she first died, do you think I didn't grieve like anyone else? But I looked back to her beginning and the time before she was born. Not only the time before she was born, but the time before she had a body.

Not only the time before she had a body, but the time before she had a spirit. In the midst of the jumble of wonder and mystery a change took place and she had a spirit. Another change and she had a body. Another change and she was born. Now there's been another change and she's dead. It's just like the progression of the four seasons, spring, summer, fall, winter. Now she's going to lie down peacefully in a vast room. If I were to follow after her bawling and sobbing, it would show that I don't understand anything about fate. So I stopped."

TAOISM: CHUANG TZU

IMPERSONAL SURVIVAL

Some spiritual traditions suggest an impersonal survival of death. Jewish scripture tells us that King David lived on after his death through the good deeds of his son. A Mali poem sees the dead as having become a part of nature. They continue to exist in the sounds of the wind, in the wailing of children, in the rocks and forest. They are not dead, they are alive everywhere.

The Rabbis ask: "Why does the Bible in recording David's death, say: 'And David slept with his fathers?' Why does it not say: 'And David died?'" "Because," replied the Sages, "David left a son who walked in the good ways of his father, and who continued his noble deeds; therefore, David was really not dead, but lived on through the good deeds of his son."

JUDAISM: BABA BATRA 116A

RIGHT
The Indian Widow,
*Joseph Wright of
Derby.*

*Those who are dead are never gone:
they are there
in the thickening shadow.
The dead are not under the earth:
they are there in the tree that rustles,
they are in the wood that groans,
they are in the water that runs,
they are in the water that sleeps,
they are in the hut,
they are in the crowd,
the dead are not dead.*

*Those who are dead are never gone:
they are in the breast of the woman,
they are in the child who is wailing,
and in the firebrand that flames.
The dead are not under the earth:
they are in the fire that is dying,
they are in the grasses that weep,
they are in the whimpering rocks,
they are in the forest,
they are in the house,
the dead are not dead.*

INDIGENOUS RELIGIONS: BIRAGO DIOP,
MALI POEM

SURVIVAL OF THE SOUL

Most religions teach that although the body dies, the consciousness which inhabited it does not. Death is not extinction, but the beginning of a new life. Jewish scripture sees death as the end of the battle with our impulse to sin and the entrance to a sinless world. The body is a burden from which death releases us. The Qur'an sees the natural return of life to the barren earth when the rain comes as a sign from Allah of the reality of our own continuation after death.

Just as the womb takes in and gives forth again, so the grave takes in and will give forth again.
Death is very good because it takes man to a sinless world, where the battle with his impulses is ended. The mystics conceived of the body as an encumbering garment which falls away at death and leaves the true man free to rise into the light of the heavenly life.

JUDAISM: BERAKOT 1 5B; BERESHIT RABBAH 9; ZAHAR TO TERUMAH

And among His signs is this: you see the earth barren and desolate, but when He sends down rain to it, it is stirred to life and yields increase. Truly, He who gives life to the dead earth can surely give life to men who are dead. For He has power over all things.

ISLAM: QUR'AN 41.39

LEFT
Journey of the sun god Khnum in a barque towed by Uraeue in the Underworld of Osiris, Egyptian funerary stele.

INCARNATION

Materialist science teaches that consciousness is a product of the human brain and when the body dies consciousness ends. Spirituality, however, teaches that consciousness survives death because a human being is not a conscious body, but consciousness incarnate. The body is a mortal shell which contains or expresses immortal consciousness. The modern Japanese religion Seicho-no-le describes the body as a cocoon built from threads of mind which enclose the soul. A soul escapes the body at death just as a butterfly flies free from its cocoon. This image was also used by the ancient Greeks who called the soul *psyche*, which also means "butterfly."

Rather than focusing on the fear of death, the writings attributed to the ancient pagan sage Hermes Trismegistus describes the fear of birth experienced by souls awaiting incarnation. They despair at being exiled from their celestial home, and moan and shriek with fear at the prospect of their earthly fate. It is birth, not death, which is terrifying. Birth is incarceration. Death is liberation. When our term as guardians of this world is done, we return, cleansed and purified, to our original higher nature. Birth is not the beginning of life, and death is not the end. It is only ignorance of this fact that creates fear of death.

RIGHT
Various incarnations of Buddha.

*M*an's real nature
is primarily spiritual life,
which weaves its threads of mind
to build a cocoon of flesh,
encloses its own soul in the cocoon,
and, for the first time,
the spirit becomes flesh.
Understand this clearly:
the cocoon is not the silkworm;
in the same way, the physical body is
not man but merely man's cocoon.
Just as the silkworm will break out of
its cocoon and fly free,
so, too, will man break out of his
body-cocoon
and ascend to the spiritual world
when his time is come.
Never think that the death of the
physical body is the death of man.
Since man is life,
he will never know death.

SHINTO: SEICHO-NO-LE. NECTAREAN
SHOWER OF HOLY DOCTRINES

I have seen a vision of souls
about to be shut up in bodies.
Some of them wailed and moaned.
Some struggled against their doom,
like noble beasts
caught by crafty hunters
and dragged away
from their wild home.
One shrieked
and looking up and down exclaimed:
"O Heaven, source of Being,
bright shining stars
and unfailing sun and moon,
Light and Life-breath of the One,
all you that share our home -
how cruel it is
that we are being torn away
from such celestial splendor!
We are to be expelled
from this holy atmosphere
and from the blissful life
we live here,
to be imprisoned
in a mean and sorry place.
What hard necessities wait for us?
What hateful thing
will we have to do
to meet the needs of a body
that will quickly perish?
And when we hear
our brothers and sisters
blowing with the wind
we shall grieve
that we are no longer breathing
in unison with them."

Birth is not the beginning of life –
only of an individual awareness.
Change into another state
is not death –
only the ending of this awareness.
Most people are ignorant
of the Truth,
and therefore afraid of death,
believing it to be the greatest
of all evils.
But death is only the dissolution
of a worn out body.
Our term of service
as guardians of the world
is ended when we are freed
from the bonds of this mortal frame
and restored,
cleansed and purified,
to the primal condition
of our higher nature.

ANCIENT MYSTERY RELIGIONS: HERMETICA

LEFT
The green Tara,
Buddhist goddess.

REINCARNATION

Hindus, Buddhists, ancient pagans, most indigenous traditions, and sects in all religions, teach the doctrine of reincarnation. They believe that after a brief sojourn in the realms beyond death, a soul takes a new human birth. It reincarnates as another being to continue its journey of spiritual evolution. The Hindu Srimad Bhagavatam describes the moment of death, when a soul sees its past life flash before its awareness. This experience has been related by many modern people who have died physically for a short while and returned to tell the tale – the so-called Near-Death Experience. Life review is often described as a sort of self-judgment, when the soul is aware of all it has done and been, and of all the consequences of its thoughts and actions.

The pagan sage Empedocles writes, "For already I have once been a boy and a girl, a bird, and a dumb sea fish" (Fragment 117). This is an example of transmigration, also expressed by the Sufi poet Rumi. It holds that a consciousness evolves through many incarnations starting with primitive forms of life, before finally achieving a human birth, which gives it the opportunity to awaken fully and become enlightened. A life well lived advances the soul on this ladder of evolution, while a bad life may lead to slipping backwards and reincarnating as an animal. Someone who has realized God in this life does not reincarnate at all. Their journey is done, and they no longer need a physical body within which to evolve.

For thousands and thousands of years I existed as a rock.
Then I died and became a plant.
For thousands and thousands of years I existed as a plant.
Then I died and became a fish.
For thousands and thousands of years I existed as fish.
Then I died and became an animal.
For thousands and thousands of years I existed as an animal.
Then I died
and became a human being.
Tell me,
what have I ever lost by dying?

ISLAM: SUFI MASTER RUMI

Priests and priestesses of the sort who make it their business to be able to account for the functions which they perform, talk of it. Pindar speaks of it too, and many other poets who are divinely inspired. What they say is this – see whether you think they are speaking the truth. They say that the soul of man is immortal. At one time it comes to an end – that which is called death – and at another is born again, but is never finally exterminated. The soul, since it is immortal and has been born many times, and has seen all things both here and in the other world, has learned everything that is.

ANCIENT MYSTERY RELIGIONS: PLATO, MENO

At the moment of death the sum of all the experiences of life on earth comes to the surface of the mind – for in the mind are stored all impressions of past deeds – and the dying man then becomes absorbed in these experiences. Then comes complete loss of memory. Next there arises before man's mind the vision of his life to come, a vision regulated by his impressions of his past deeds; and he no longer recollects his life on earth. This complete forgetfulness of his past identity is death.

His complete acceptance of another state and identification with a new body is said to be his birth. He no longer remembers his past life, and, though he has existed before, he considers himself newly born.

His next birth is regulated by the deeds of the present life – the deeds which make up his character. If his character is dominated by light, he achieves a higher birth, that of a deva or of a sage; if by passion, he is returned to earth as a demon or as a man; and if by darkness he is born from the lower wombs.

HINDUISM: SRIMAD BHAGAVATAM 11.15

LEFT
The cycles of reincarnation.

THE TIBETAN BOOK OF THE DEAD

The Tibetan Book of the Dead is a remarkable Buddhist guide to the dying process. It teaches that death is an opportunity to attain enlightenment. It is read to a dying person while they are in the process of leaving the body. The soul is guided towards the Clear Light of the Void which awaits it in the bardo state after death. If it recognizes the light as the pure consciousness of its own Buddha Nature, it is freed from rebirth in one of the after-death realms and eventual earthly reincarnation. It becomes "en-lightened."

The light is described as "void" because it is consciousness conscious of nothing. Only a mature soul is able to experience the emptiness of the void – the Self only conscious of itself – without falling unconscious. Immature souls simply black out. They reawaken in a bardo realm, heavenly or hellish, before being propelled by their karma to take human rebirth.

O nobly-born (so and so by name), the time has now come for you to seek the Path in reality. Your breathing is about to cease. Your guru has set you face to face before with the Clear Light; and now you are about to experience it in its Reality in the Bardo state, wherein all things are like the void and cloudless sky, and the naked, spotless intellect is like a transparent vacuum without circumference or center. At this moment, know your Self; and abide in that state. I, too, at this time, am setting you face to face.

O nobly-born (so-and-so), listen. Now you are experiencing the Radiance of the Clear Light of Pure Reality. Recognize it. O nobly-born, your present intellect, in real nature void, not formed into anything as regards characteristics or color, naturally void, is the very Reality, the All-Good.

Your own intellect, which is now voidness, yet not to be regarded as of the voidness of nothingness but as being the intellect itself; unobstructed, shining, thrilling, and blissful, is the very Consciousness, the All-good Buddha.

Your own consciousness, not formed into anything, in reality void, and the intellect, shining and blissful – these two are inseparable. The union of them is the Dharma-Kaya state of Perfect Enlightenment.

Your own consciousness, shining, void, and inseparable from the Great Body of Radiance, has no birth, nor death, and is the Immutable Light - Buddha Amitabha.

Knowing this is sufficient. Recognizing the voidness of thine own intellect to be Buddhahood, and looking upon it as being thine own consciousness, is to keep yourself in the state of the divine mind of the Buddha.

BUDDHISM: TIBETAN BOOK OF THE DEAD

LEFT
One of the keepers of the gate of heaven, Buddhist.

TRANSCENDING LIFE AND DEATH

According to the mystical traditions, in all religions, the Ultimate Truth lies beyond either life or death in an awareness of consciousness itself, which experiences both.

A Buddhist story tells of a man who hears a fragment of the true teaching that everything is impermanent and changing. He longs to hear more, but must first be prepared to offer himself up completely. Only when he is willing to die are the teachings completed and he understands that there is something that transcends both life and death. Yet he does not die, but is received by a radiant god. In this story, the teachings are revealed by a god who has disguised himself as a demon to test the sincerity of the seeker's resolve to find the truth. This tale is a metaphor for the world in which we live; it teaches us that everything is impermanent, including ourselves. Only when we understand and genuinely accept this truth are the rest of the teachings revealed to us so we can know that which never changes – Consciousness the eternal witness of all. We then discover that, far from experiencing extinction, we know our true immortal nature.

Chuang Tzu explains that transitory impermanent things come into being and cease to be within space and time, but space and time are themselves permanent and unchanging. Pure Consciousness does not exist within space and time, but like space has unlimited existence, and like time has eternal continuity. Consciousness comes into a temporal personal existence at birth and leaves at death. That through which it comes and goes has no form. It is "the Portal of God." It is the experiencer, the witness, the "I am" – the self.

RIGHT
Fatima receives a parcel of the green cloak brought by Gabriel from paradise, in the presence of Muhammad.

Birth is not a beginning; death is not an end. There is existence without limitation; there is continuity without a starting point. Existence without limitation is space. Continuity without a starting point is time. There is birth, there is death, there is issuing forth, there is entering in. That through which one passes in and out without seeing its form, that is the Portal of God.

TAOISM: CHUANG TZU 23, P.234

*God does not die,
I will therefore not die.*

INDIGENOUS RELIGIONS: AKAN PROVERB
FROM GHANA

*O*nce there was a person who sought the True Path in the Himalayas. He cared nothing for all the treasures of the earth or even for all the delights of heaven, but he sought the teaching that would remove all mental delusions. The gods were impressed by the man's earnestness and sincerity and decided to test his mind. So one of the gods disguised himself as a demon and appeared in the Himalayas, singing,
"Everything changes.
Everything appears
and disappears."
The seeker heard this song which pleased him, as if he had found a spring of cool water for his thirst or as if he were a slave unexpectedly set free. He thought, "At last I have found the true teaching that I have sought for so long." He followed the voice and at last came upon the frightful demon. With an uneasy mind he approached the demon and said, "Was it you who sang the holy song that I have just heard? If it was you, please sing more of it." The demon replied, "Yes, it was my song, but I can not sing more of it until I

have had something to eat; I am starving." The man begged him in earnest, saying, "It has a sacred meaning to me and I have sought its teaching for a long time. I have only heard a part of it; please let me hear more." The demon said again, "I am starving, but if I can taste the warm flesh and blood of a man, I will finish the song." The man, in his eagerness to hear the teaching, promised the demon that he could have his body after he had heard the teaching. Then the demon sang the complete song,
"Everything changes.
Everything appears and disappears.
There is perfect tranquility
when one transcends
both life and extinction."
Hearing this, the man, after he wrote the poem on rocks and trees around, quietly climbed a tree and hurled himself to the feet of the demon, but the demon had disappeared and, instead, a radiant god received the body of the man unharmed.

BUDDHISM: MAHAPARINIRVANA SUTRA

424–33

ABOVE
Abraham and the angels, Book of Hours of Alfonso of Aragon, *Italian, 1480.*

TOP
The Ascension of Christ, *Giotto (1276-1337).*

LEFT
The Angel of
Revelation, *William
Blake (1757-1827)*.

CHAPTER TEN

The Sage

SCRIPTURE POINTS TO A DOORWAY into an intuitive, spiritual understanding of the mysteries of life and death. What are the qualities of the someone who has walked through this open entrance to enlightenment? Although different religious traditions use different language and emphasize different qualities, they agree on the essential characteristics of such a being.

Sages are selfless. They have transcended their personal selves and discovered the Universal Self. They follow God's will and have no will of their own. They accept whatever happens. They have no personal agenda, so know neither failure nor success. They see others as part of God and so are nonjudgmental and compassionate. They witness the omnipresent evolution of consciousness and therefore do not see good and evil, but only a continual striving from ignorance to knowledge. They live as spontaneously as a child. They are natural human beings, in harmony with life.

Enlightened sages are only temporary residents of earth, like the rest of us. Yet they do not believe they are only a mortal body and personality, but know themselves to be the eternal consciousness which inhabits it. Such beings are not with personality. Usually they are full of color, humor, and individuality. They are individuals, but not separate from God.

Enlightened sages are the fulfillment of God's creation. They are what we could be. They are living testimony to the truth contained in sacred scripture. Through simply being in their presence, we too can awaken the innate natural goodness of our true self. Zen master Ikkyu writes, "One glimpse of the true human being and we are in love." We are in love with such beings because they are love. When you glimpse the true human being that resides inside yourself, you will also fall in love and dissolve into God.

THE SOCIETY OF SAINTS

The great sages and saints of all traditions are embodiments of the truth they teach. They inspire us by their example. Hindus say that by experiencing *darshan* – being in the presence of a spiritually evolved being – we can ourselves partake of something of their wisdom by a sort of spiritual osmosis. Scripture advises us to seek out such teachers and the fellowship of other seekers, which Buddhists call the *sangha* and Hindus *satsanga* – the company of truth. This is an environment conducive to our spiritual evolution, in which all participants become enriched.

*One not knowing a land asks of one
who knows it, he goes forward
instructed by the knowing one. Such,
indeed, is the blessing of instruction,
one finds a path that leads him
straight onward.*

HINDUISM: RIG VEDA 10.32.7

*The Master said, "Only one who
bursts with eagerness do I instruct;
only one who bubbles with
excitement do I enlighten. If I hold
up one corner and a man cannot come
back to me with the other three, I do
not continue the lesson."*

*The Master said, "Even when
walking in a party of no more than
three I can always be certain of
learning from those I am with. There
will be good qualities that I can select
for imitation and bad ones that will
teach me what requires correction
in myself."*

CONFUCIANISM: ANALECTS 7.8 AND 7.21

*Just as cold disappears
by sitting near the fire,
So are sins destroyed in the
congregation of saints.
Now, I am jealous of no one,*

*Now that I have attained
unto the society of the saints:
I am estranged with no one:
nor is anyone a stranger to me,
Indeed, I am the friend of all.
All that God does,
with that I am pleased;
This is the wisdom I have received
from the saints.
The One God pervades all:
and, seeing Him,
I am wholly in bloom.*

SIKHISM: ADI GRANTH,
RAMKALI ASHTPADI, M. 5

*Much Torah have I learned from
my teachers, more from my
colleagues, but from my students most
of all.*

JUDAISM: TAANIT 7A

AN EMBODIMENT OF GOD

Masters are often seen as embodiments of God. They are one with God. The Hindu Kularnava Tantra explains that Shiva (God) takes the form of a guru out of compassion for us, because in himself he is ineffable and so difficult for us to relate to. The master is a tangible form with which we may have a relationship, and so come to know God. To the foolish, the teacher appears to be just a human being, but the wise see God in him. A master who has no separate self knows he is an expression of the Oneness of God. When he speaks, he knows that it is God speaking. His words and teachings are the words of God, undistorted by any separate ego. When he says "I" he is not referring to his particular personality, but the universal Consciousness which inhabits it.

Many of Jesus' teachings which are misunderstood as claims that he is the only way to God, are actually teachings about this universal "I." Neil Douglas-Klotz points out that in the Aramaic of the Peshitta gospels, the word that Jesus uses is *inana*, which literally means the "I of I." It is an intensification of the word "I" which signifies its distilled essence. Jesus is pointing beyond his own personality to the "I am" of impersonal Pure Consciousness.

The common translations of Jesus' words from the Greek versions of the Gospels miss the depth and many resonances of his original meaning. For example, the phrase usually translated "I am the good shepherd" (John 10:11), conveys in the Aramaic "The peaceful center at the middle of 'Who am I' leads our anxieties to the right pasture at the right moment." The phrase "I am the door" (John 8:12) conveys "Simple presence shuttles back and forth from limitation to freedom." The phrase "I am the truth and the life" (John 14:6) conveys "The 'I am' is the path, the sense of true direction, and the life force to travel." Jesus is not teaching us that he is God's only representative, but that no one comes to the Father but via the "I am" – the ineffable eternal consciousness that inhabits each one of us.

BELOW
The Martyrdom of the disciple St. Andrew, German, 10th century.

*G*lory be to Lord Mahavira, in whose mirror of enlightenment are reflected vividly the terrestrial and the extra-terrestrial, and whose complexion resembles the interior of a blooming lotus and burnished gold.

JAINISM: VIRASENA, JAYADHAVALA 3

*The guru, it is declared, is the very
Lord himself. To approach the guru,
to worship the guru, is to approach
the Lord, worship the Lord. Why
should the Lord choose to manifest
through the guru, why should he not
act directly?
Shiva is really all-pervading, above
the mind, without features,
imperishable, infinite; how can such a
one be worshiped? That is why, out of
compassion for his creatures, He takes
the form of the guru and, when so
worshiped in devotion, grants
liberation and fulfillment. Shiva has
no binding form, Shiva is not
perceivable by the human eye;
therefore He protects the disciple
conforming to Dharma in the form of
the guru. The guru is none other than
the supreme Shiva enclosed in human
skin; he walks the earth, concealed,
bestowing grace on the good disciples.
To him who is loaded with sinful
karma, the guru appears to be
human; but to him whose karma is
auspicious, meritful, the guru appears
as Shiva.*

HINDUISM: KULARNAVA TANTRA 13

*Jesus said to them,
"Truly, truly, I say to you,
before Abraham was, I am.
Do you not know me, Philip?
He who has seen me has seen
the Father;
how can you say,
'Show us the Father?'
Do you not believe that
I am in the Father and the
Father in me?"*

CHRISTIANITY: JOHN 8.58

AND 14.9–10

*Whoever sees me, Muhammad,
has seen God.*

ISLAM: HADITH OF BUKHARI AND MUSLIM

*Jesus said "I am he who exists
from the undivided."
Jesus said "It is I who am the light
which is above them all. It is I who
am the all. From me did the all come
forth, and unto me did the all extend.
Split a piece of wood, and I am there.
Lift up the stone, and you will find
me there."*

CHRISTIANITY: GOSPEL OF THOMAS

61 AND 77

*Says Nanak,
"The Master is the Lord's image;
The Lord totally fills the Master.
Brother! There is no difference
between them."*

SIKHISM: ADI GRANTH, ASA CHHANT, M.4

ONLY A MORTAL

As well as speaking of themselves as God, the great masters also affirm that they are merely mortals. Their essential nature is divine and immortal, but their particular form, like all others, is limited and transitory. Jesus repudiates a man who calls him good, because only God is good. The Buddhist master Shinran describes himself as totally ignorant. The Qur'an advises us not to associate anyone with the Lord's service. If the disciple identifies God with the person of the master, the disciple has missed the point. God is the impersonal consciousness which exists in master and pupil. The master is aware of this, but the student is not. The great task of masters is to guide their disciples to the same awareness that they themselves enjoy. To do this, they at times emphasize their oneness with God, and at other times point out that they too are mere mortals.

A man ran up and knelt before Jesus and asked him, "Good Teacher, what must I do to gain eternal life?" And Jesus said to him, "Why do you call me good? No one is good but God alone."

CHRISTIANITY: MARK 10.17–18

*Say, I do not say to you, "I possess the treasuries of God;" I know not the Unseen. And I say not to you, "I am an angel;" I only follow what is revealed to me.
Say, I am only a mortal the like of you; it is revealed to me that God is One. So let him who hopes for the encounter with his Lord work righteousness, and not associate with his Lord's service anyone.*

ISLAM: QUR'AN 6.50 AND 18.110

Zendo says "We must realize that each of us is an ordinary mortal, immersed in sin and crime, subject to birth and death, ceaselessly migrating from all eternity and ever sinking deeper into hell, without any means of delivering ourselves from it." It was on this account that Shinran most graciously used himself as an example, in order to make us realize how lost every single one of us is and how we fail to appreciate our personal indebtedness to the grace of Amida. In truth, none of us mentions the great love of Amida, but we continually talk about what is good and what is bad. Shinran said, however, "Of good and evil I am totally ignorant. If I understood good as Buddha understands it, then I could say I knew what was good. If I understood evil as Buddha understands it, then I could say I knew what was bad. But I am an ordinary mortal, full of passion and desire, living in this transient world like the dweller in a house on fire. Every judgment of mine, whatever I say, is nonsense and gibberish."

BUDDHISM: THE SAYINGS OF SHINRAN

THE AZTEC SAGE

The Spaniard Bernardino de Sahagun recorded from the Aztecs their traditional view of the qualities of a wise human being. Such a one embodies the spiritual path. They help others find their "face." They are like a mirror within which others can see their true nature. They comfort and heal everyone.

The wise man: a light, a torch, a stout torch that does not smoke.
A perforated mirror, a mirror pierced on both sides.
His are the black and red ink, his are the illustrated manuscripts, he studies the illustrated manuscripts.
He himself is writing and wisdom.
He is the path, the true way for others.
He directs people and things; he is a guide in human affairs.
The wise man is careful like a physician and preserves tradition.
His is the handed-down wisdom; he teaches it; he follows the path of truth.
Teacher of the truth, he never ceases to admonish.
He makes wise the countenances of others; to them he gives a face; he leads them to develop it.
He opens their ears; he enlightens them.
He is the teacher of guides; he shows them their path.
One depends upon him.
He puts a mirror before others; he makes them prudent, cautious; he causes a face to appear in them.
He attends to things; he regulates their path, he arranges and commands.

He applies his light to the world.
He knows what is above us and in the region of the dead.
He is a serious man.
Everyone is comforted by him, corrected, taught.
Thanks to him people humanize their will and receive a strict education.
He comforts the heart, he comforts the people, he helps, gives remedies, heals everyone.

ANCIENT AZTEC RELIGION: BERNARDINO DE SAHAGUN, CODICE MATRITEUSE DE LA REAL ACADEMIA DE LA HISTORIA

LEFT
Figure of the god Quetzacoatl, Mexican, c. 1570.

THE JEWISH SAGE

In Jewish writings the wise human being is called a *Zaddik*. The whole world was created to allow the possibility of such enlightened sages. They rule over God, because they can annul God's decrees since they have become free from the prison of fate. They are humble, strong, and compassionate. Yet although they sustain the world, they are not sustained by their own merit, but by God.

The soul of one Zaddik has the weight and importance of the entire world.
The whole world was created only for the sake of the righteous man. He weighs as much as the whole world. The whole world was created only to be united to him.
Even if a decree has issued from God, the Zaddik can annul it.
"I rule over man," says God. "Who rules over Me? The Zaddik. I decree and he annuls."
The prayers of the Zaddikim turn God's nature from anger to compassion.
The Zaddikim say little and do much. The more honors the Zaddikim receive, the more humble they become.
He hears himself abused, and yet keeps silent.
The world is sustained by the merit of the Zaddikim, but the Zaddikim are not sustained by their own merit.
The true Zaddik is not like Noah, who heard of the doom of the world and did not pray for the doomed;
but like Abraham, who heard of the doom of Sodom and immediately prayed for its inhabitants.
The ideal man has the strength of a male and the compassion of a female.
God wishes to honor the Zaddik more than he wishes honor for Himself.

JUDAISM: SANHEDRIN 103; SHABBAT 30B AND 63; MOED KATON 16; YEBAMOT 64; HULLIN 7; PESIKTA ZUTARTI TO BEMIDBAR; YALKUT TO PSALMS 629; BERAKOT 17; ZOHAR I 254B, IV 145B, AND V 288A.

RIGHT
The Prophet Micah, *André Beauneveu* (c. 1335-1410).

THE HINDU SAGE

In the Bhagavad Gita, Krishna describes the qualities of a perfect devotee. Such a one no longer has any sense of "me" and "mine." They are detached, selfless, and equanimous. The Ashtavakra Gita describes the wise as accepting the naturalness of birth and death, happiness and misery. They have no desires and so no anxiety. They know that they are Pure Consciousness and have no personal will. They are free from concepts that divide up the oneness of things, and so see themselves in all – from Brahma (God the Creator) to a blade of grass. They experience this world as samsara – a wonderful illusion. They are not attached to this illusion and so have no desire to be free from it. They live contentedly within samsara, watching everything come and go. The Kularnava Tantra explains that such sages may appear uncivil or ignorant. They may act like a fool or speak like a drunk. They take on different disguises as is necessary. They play on the earth out of compassion for all people.

Living beyond the reach of "I" and "mine" and of pleasure and pain, patient, contented, self controlled, firm in faith, with all his heart and all his mind given to me – with such a one I am in love.
Not frightening the world or by it frightened, he stands above the sway of elation, competition, and fear – he is my beloved.
He is detached, pure, efficient, impartial, never anxious, selfless in all his undertakings – he is my devotee, very dear to me.
Running not after the pleasant or away from the painful, grieving not, lusting not, but letting things come and go as they happen – he is very dear to me.
That devotee who looks upon friend and foe with equal regard, who is not buoyed up by praise nor cast down by blame, alike in heat and cold, pleasure and pain, free from selfish attachments, the same in honor and dishonor, quiet, ever full, in harmony everywhere, firm in faith – such a one is dear to me.

Those who meditate upon this immortal Truth as I have declared it, full of faith and seeking me as life's supreme goal, are truly my devotees, and my love for them is very great.

HINDUISM: BHAGAVAD GITA 12.14–20

LEFT
Ladies visiting a yogini, Indian.

In the conviction that happiness and misery, birth, and death are parts of the natural process of causality, the man of wisdom, without any need to accomplish anything, is free from anxiety and does not identify himself with anything he happens to be doing.

In the conviction that it is anxiety and nothing else that is the root cause of misery in this world, the man of wisdom, with his desires annihilated, remains free from anxiety, happy, and contented.

In the conviction "I am not the body, nor is the body mine – I am pure Consciousness," the man of wisdom is indifferent to what has been achieved and what remains to be achieved, and lives in a natural state of non-volition.

In the conviction "I am immanent in all phenomena, from Brahma to a blade of grass," the man of wisdom is free from any conceptualizing or objectifying, indifferent to what has been attained or not attained, and remains contented and at peace.

In the conviction that this manifested universe, wondrous though it be in the variety and diversity of its phenomena, is truly illusory, the man of wisdom, without any desires, identified with the pure Consciousness, remains in noumenal peace.

One who is attached to samsara wants to renounce it in order to free himself from misery. But one who is not attached continues to remain in samsara and yet live happily.

HINDUISM: ASHTAVAKRA GITA 102–6
AND 154

Adepts in yoga speak in the manner of the uncivil, behave as if ignorant, appear like the lowly. They do so in order that men may ignore them and not flock to them; they talk nothing at all. Though realized in freedom, the yogi will sport like a child, may conduct himself like a dullard, talk like one intoxicated. Such a yogi lives in a way that this world of men may laugh, feel disgust, revile, and seeing, pass at a distance, leaving him alone.

He would go about in different guises, at times like one worthy, at times like one fallen, at times like a ghost or demon. If the yogi accepts things of life it is for the good of the world and not out of desire. Out of compassion for all men, he will sport on the earth.

HINDUISM: KULARNAVA TANTRA 9

RIGHT
*Buddhist thanka,
19th-20th century.*

THE BUDDHIST SAGE

The Dhammapada, a scripture of the Theravada Buddhist school, describes the perfect Brahmin – the servant of Brahman (God) – as having traveled from the ignorance of separation to the further shore of enlightenment. Now all is one, so there is neither this shore nor that shore, nor both. He has realized his Buddha Nature that has always been enlightened. He has arrived where he, unknowingly, has always been.

In the Mahayana Buddhist tradition, the ideal is the Bodhisattva – one who forgoes final enlightenment to reincarnate out of compassion for all sentient beings, so that he or she may help them also reach the truth. The Mahaparinirvana Sutra teaches that Bodhisattvas are like caring parents whose hearts ache for their children. They are always concerned with relieving the sufferings of others. They are all love.

When beyond meditation and contemplation a Brahmin has reached the other shore, then he attains the supreme vision and all his fetters are broken.
He for whom there is neither this nor the further shore, nor both, who, beyond all fear, is free –
him I call a Brahmin.
He who hurts not with his thoughts, or words or deeds, who keeps these three under control –
him I call a Brahmin.
Who, though innocent, suffers insults, stripes and chains, whose weapons are endurance and soul-force –
him I call a Brahmin.
Who clings not to sensuous pleasures, even as water clings not to the leaf of the lotus, or a grain of mustard seed to the point of a needle –
him I call a Brahmin.
He who even in this life knows the end of sorrow, who has laid down his burden and is free –
him I call a Brahmin.
Who hurts not any living being, whether feeble or strong, who neither kills nor causes to kill –
him I call a Brahmin.
Who is tolerant to the intolerant, peaceful to the violent, free from greed with the greedy –
him I call a Brahmin.

He who speaks words that are peaceful and useful and true, words that offend no one –
him I call a Brahmin.
He who in this world has gone beyond good and evil and both, who free from sorrows is free from passions and is pure –
him I call a Brahmin.
He who is free from pleasure and pain, who is calm, and whose seeds of death-in-life are burnt, whose heroism has conquered all the inner worlds – him I call a Brahmin.
He who knows the going and returning of beings – the birth and rebirth of life – and in joy has arrived at the end of his journey, and now he is awake and can see –
him I call a Brahmin.
He for whom things future or past or present are nothing, who has nothing and desires nothing –
him I call a Brahmin.
He who is powerful, noble, who lives a life of inner heroism, the all-seer, the all-conqueror, the ever-pure, who has reached the end of the journey, who like Buddha is awake –
him I call a Brahmin.

BUDDHISM: DHAMMAPADA

The Bodhisattva is a great being who practices compassion, sympathy, and joy, and so attains the stage of the "beloved only child." Parents are very happy when they see their son at peace. The Bodhisattva, who has reached this stage, sees all beings like a parent sees his only son – seeing him practising goodness, the parent is delighted.

Hence the name of this stage.

A father's or mother's heart is troubled when their son is ill. Empathy fills them, and they can't stop thinking about the illness. It is the same with the Bodhisattva who rests in this stage. When he sees any being enmeshed in the illness of illusion, his heart aches. He is as concerned as if it were his only son.

When a child picks up earth, dirty things, tiles, stones, old bones, pieces of wood and puts them into his mouth, his parents are worried that he will hurt himself and taking the child with one hand they remove the item with the other. The Bodhisattva does the same. He sees that all beings are not mature and that they act misguidedly in body, speech, and mind. With the hand of wisdom he saves them from their misguidedness,

because he does not wish that they should repeat birth and death, and so receiving more suffering and anxiety.

When a beloved son dies, his parents' hearts ache so much that they want to die themselves as well. It is the same with the Bodhisattva. When he sees an unfortunate person fall into hell, he too wants to be born there. He thinks, "Perhaps as this person suffers he may repent for a moment and I can teach him about the Dharma in some way, and so help him to have good thoughts."

Whether asleep or awake, or while walking, standing, sitting, or resting, the mind of a mother or father is always on their son. If he acts badly, they give kindly advice to guide him so that he does not do so again. It is the same with the Bodhisattva. He sees beings fall into the hell-realms of hungry ghosts and animals. He watches them acting well or badly both in heaven and the world of men. His attention is always with them. Even if he sees them only committing evil, he is not angry and does not maliciously punish them.

BUDDHISM: MAHAPARINIRVANA SUTRA

470–71

THE ORIENTAL SAGE

Confucius describes the good human being as humble, respectful, non-judgmental, and as having integrity. Lao Tzu sees the ancient masters as having such unfathomable depths that only their outer appearance is capable of being described. They are simple, unpretentious, and empty of self. Chuang Tzu was honored with the title "Nan Hua Chen Jen" – "The True Person of Hua." He describes the true human being as totally accepting of life. His mind is like a perfect mirror which adds nothing of its own to distort reality, but reflects the truth perfectly. He is not concerned about the judgments of others and so does not react to praise or blame. He is one with the harmony of life – the Tao.

Confucius said, "The good man does not grieve that other people do not recognize his merits. His only anxiety is lest he should fail to recognize theirs."
Tzu-kung asked about the true gentleman. The Master said, "He does not preach what he practices until he has practiced what he preaches."
Confucius said, "The gentleman calls attention to the good points in others; he does not call attention to their defects. The small man does just the reverse of this."

CONFUCIANISM:

ANALECTS 1.16, 2.13 AND 12.16

The Ancient Masters understood Mystery The depths of their wisdom were unfathomable, so all we have are descriptions of how they looked... Careful, as if crossing a frozen river. Alert, as if aware of danger. Respectful, like a guest. Yielding, like melting ice. Simple, like uncarved wood. Empty, like a valley.

TAOISM: TAO TE CHING 15

RIGHT
A scribe or apostle writing, from The Four Gospels, *by the monk Spiridione, Romanian, 1503.*

What do I mean by a True Man? The True Man of ancient times did not rebel against want, did not grow proud in plenty, and did not plan his affairs. Being like this, he could commit an error and not regret it, could meet with success and not make a show. Being like this, he could climb the high places and not be frightened, could enter the water and not get wet, could enter the fire and not get burned. His knowledge was able to climb all the way up to the Tao like this.

The True Man of ancient times knew nothing of loving life, knew nothing of hating death. He emerged without delight; he went back in without a fuss. He came briskly, he went briskly, and that was all. He did not forget where he began; he did not try to find out where he would end. He received something and took pleasure in it; he forgot about it and handed it back again. This is what I call not using the mind to repel the Tao, not using man to help out Heaven.
This is what I call the True Man.

The mind of the perfect man is like a mirror. It does not lean forward or backward in its response to things. It responds to things but conceals nothing of its own. Therefore it is able to deal with things without injury to its reality.
The Man of the Tao wins no fame. The highest virtue wins no gain. The Great Man has no self.
The man who has had his feet cut off in punishment discards his fancy clothes – because praise and blame no longer touch him. The chained convict climbs the highest peak without fear – because he has abandoned all thought of life and death. These two are submissive and unashamed because they have forgotten other men, and by forgetting other men they have become men of Heaven. You may treat such men with respect, but they will not be pleased; you may treat them with contempt, but they will not be angry. Only because they are one with the Heavenly Harmony can they be like this.

BELOW
The Aged Mullah, Mughal miniature, c. 1610.

I have no corporeal existence, but Universal Benevolence is my divine body. I have no physical power, but Uprightness is my strength. I have no religious clairvoyance beyond what is bestowed by Wisdom, I have no power of miracle other than the attainment of quiet happiness, I have no tact except the exercise of gentleness.

BEYOND DESCRIPTION

Despite all of these descriptions, enlightened sages remain an enigma. Like God, they are ultimately beyond description. In the Gospel of Thomas, Jesus asks his disciples who they think he is. Thomas cannot begin to put into words what he perceives in Jesus. Jesus recognizes in this inarticulate response a great depth of understanding. Thomas is no longer his student, for he has become like Jesus. The hidden things have been revealed to him. The Buddha, likewise, dismisses all descriptions of himself – even that of being human. He is simply "Buddha," the witnessing consciousness, and nothing more may be said.

The Diamond Sutra points out that enlightened beings cannot even say to themselves that they are enlightened, for this would involve the idea of a self. Enlightenment happens in the process of spiritual evolution, but it does not create an enlightened person, for enlightenment is the complete understanding that there is no self – there is only the Oneness of God. Enlightenment is an impersonal happening, not a personal achievement.

Jesus said to his disciples, "Compare me to someone and tell me who I am like."
Simon Peter said to him, "You are like a righteous angel."
Matthew said to him, "You are like a wise philosopher."
Thomas said to him, "Master, my mouth is wholly incapable of saying whom you are like."
Jesus said, "I am not your master. Because you have drunk, you have become intoxicated from the bubbling spring which I have measured out."
Jesus said, "He who will drink from my mouth will become like me. I myself shall become he, and the things that are hidden will be revealed to him ."

CHRISTIANITY:
GOSPEL OF THOMAS 13 AND 108

Subhuti, what do you think? Does a holy one say within himself, "I have obtained Perfect Enlightenment?"
Subhuti replied, "No, Worldhonored One. If a holy one of Perfect Enlightenment said to himself 'Such am I,' he would necessarily partake of the idea of an ego identity, a personality, a being, a separated individuality."

BUDDHISM: DIAMOND SUTRA 9

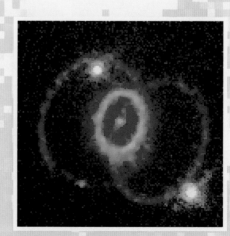

LEFT
Three rings of glowing gas around the supernova 1987A, picture taken by the Hubble telescope.

At one time the Lord was journeying along the highroad between Ukkattha and Setabbya; so also was the brahmin Dona. He saw on the Lord's footprints the wheels with their thousand spokes, their rims and hubs, and all their attributes complete, and he thought, "Indeed, how wonderful and marvelous – it cannot be that these are the footprints of a human being."
Then Dona, following the Lord's footprints, saw that he was sitting under a tree, comely, faith-inspiring, his sense-faculties and his mind peaceful. Dona approached the Lord and said, "Is your reverence a god?"
"No indeed, brahmin, I am not a god."
"Then an angel?"
"No indeed, brahmin."
"A fairy, then?"
"No indeed, brahmin, I am not a fairy."
"Then is your reverence a human being?"
"No indeed, brahmin, I am not a human being."
"You answer No to all my questions. Who then is your reverence?"

"Brahmin, those outflows whereby, if they had not been extinguished, I might have been a god, angel, fairy, or a human being – those outflows are extinguished in me, cut off at the root, made like a palm-tree stump that can come to no further existence in the future. Just as a blue, red, or white lotus, although born in the water, grown up in the water, when it reaches the surface stands there unsoiled by the water – just so, brahmin, although born in the world, grown up in the world, having overcome the world, I abide unsoiled by the world. Take it that I am Buddha."

BUDDHISM: ANGUTTARA NIKAYA II. 37–39

THE NATURALNESS OF A CHILD

The scriptures teach that the spiritual journey is one of recovering our essential divine nature. It is about progressing backwards. It is using intellectual ideas, mystical practices, and moral codes, to help us uncover our innate natural goodness. To become a sage is to become as simple and natural as a child – to play, discover, and enjoy. It is to return to a pre-conceptual awareness of the mystery and magic of life, experienced by a child before the development of its separate identity. It is living in the wonder of the oneness. It is knowledge of God, not as an idea, but as a living reality. The only reality.

Lifetime is a child at play, moving pieces in a game. Kingship belongs to the child.

ANCIENT MYSTERY RELIGIONS: HERACLITUS XCIV

Mencius said, "The great man is he who does not lose his child's heart."

CONFUCIANISM: MENCIUS IV.B.12

Activity begets attachment, abstention from activity generates aversion. Rid of the bondage of opposites, the wise man established in the Self, lives like a child.

HINDUISM: ASHTAVAKRA GITA 153

If you want to know about Natural Goodness take a look at little babies.

TAOISM: TAO TE CHING 55

BELOW
"Suffer the little children to come unto me," *Victorian painting of the life of Christ.*

The disciples asked Jesus "Who is the greatest in the kingdom of heaven?" He called a child to him and putting him in the middle of them, said, "I say to you, unless you return and become like children, you will never enter the kingdom of heaven."

CHRISTIANITY: MATTHEW 18.1–3

The simple heart finds no hard way, good thought finds no wounds. Deep in the illuminated mind is no storm. Surrounded on every side by the beauty of the open country, one is free of doubt. Below is like above. Everything is above. Below is nothing, but the ignorant think they see. Now you know grace. It is for your salvation. Believe and live and be saved.

JUDAISM: THE ODES OF SOLOMON 34

Open yourself, create free space; release the bound one from his bonds! Like a newborn child, freed from the womb, be free to move on every path!

HINDUISM: ATHARVA VEDA 6.121.4

Jesus saw infants being suckled. He said to his disciples, "These infants being suckled are like those who enter the kingdom." They said to him "Shall we then, as children, enter the kingdom?" Jesus said to them "When you make the two one and the inside like the outside and the outside like the inside, and when you make the male and the female one and the same; then you shall enter the kingdom."

CHRISTIANITY: THE GOSPEL OF THOMAS 22

God needs no pointing out to a child.

INDIGENOUS RELIGIONS: AKAN PROVERB FROM GHANA

Bibliography

A Buddhist Bible, ed. Dwight Goddard (Beacon Press, 1970)

Acarangasutra, trans. Mahendra Kumar (Motilal Barnarsidass, 1981)

A Critical Study of Adi Granath, Surindar Singh Kohli (Motilal Barnarsidass, 1961)

A Duet for One – The Ashtavakra Gita Dialogue, trans. Ramesh S. Balsekar (Advaita Press, 1989)

African Religions and Philosophy, John S. Mbiti (Heinemann, 1969)

African Religions: A Symposium, ed. Newell S. Booth (NOK Publishers, 1937)

A Guide to the Bodhisattva's Way of Life, trans. Stephen Batchelor (Library of Tibetan Works and Archives, 1979)

A Manual for Living by Epictetus, Sharon Lebell (HarperSanFrancisco, 1994)

American Indian Myths and Legends, ed. Richard Erdoes and Alfonso Ortiz (Pantheon, 1984)

Ancient Nahuatl Poetry, Daniel G. Brinton (Philadelphia, 1890)

An Anthology of Sacred Texts by and about Women, ed. Serenity Young (Crossroad, 1993)

A Prose English Translation of Agni Puranam, trans. Manmatha Nath Duff (Calcutta,1903)

A Source Book in Chinese Philosophy, trans. Wing-tsit Chan (Princeton University Press, 1963)

A Yearbook of Zen Wisdom, Timothy Freke (UK Godsfield Press/Thorsons, USA Triumph Books, 1997)

Book of the Dead, trans E.A. Wallis Budge (Kegan Paul, Trench, Trubner and Co. Ltd./E.P. Dutton and Co., 1923)

Buddhism in Translation, ed. Henry Clarke Warren (Harvard University Press, 1896)

Buddhist Texts through the Ages, ed. Edward Conze (Harper & Row, 1964)

Burning Water: Thought and Religion in Ancient Mexico, L. Séjourne (Vanguard Press, 1957)

Chuang Tzu – A New Selected Translation, Yu-Lan Fung (Commercial Press Ltd., 1933)

Chuang Tzu – Basic Writings, trans. Burton Watson (Columbia University Press, 1964)

Comparative Studies of African Traditional Religions, Emefie Ikenga-Metuh (IMICO Publishers, 1987)

Complete Works of Chuang Tzu, trans. Burton Watson (Columbia University Press, 1968)

Confucian Analects, the Great Learning and the Doctrine of the Mean, trans. James Legge (Clarendon Press, 1893)

Confucian Vision, William Mcnaughton (University of Michigan Press, 1974)

Desert Wisdom, Neil Douglas-Klotz (HarperSanFrancisco, 1995)

Discourses of Rumi, trans. A.J. Arberry (John Murray Paperbacks, 1961)

Eleusis and the Eleusinian Mysteries, trans. George E. Mylonas (Princeton University Press, 1961)

Epistle to the Son of the Wolf Baha'u'llah (National Spiritual Assembly of the Baha'is of the United States, 1941)

Essential Sacred Writings From Around the World, Mircea Eliade (HarperSanFrancisco, 1967)

Ethical Doctrines in Jainism, K.C. Sogani (Jain Sam. Samraksaka Sangha, 1967)

Further Dialogues of the Buddha, trans. Lord Chalmers (London, 1926)

Gleaning from the Writings of Baha'u'llah (National Spiritual Assembly of the Baha'is of the United States, 1976)

Heaven: An Illustrated History of the Higher Realms, Timothy Freke (UK: Godsfield Press/Thorsons, USA: Conari Press, 1996)

Hellenistic Religion: The Age of Syncreticism, trans. F.C. Grant (The Liberal Arts Press Inc., 1953)

Hermetica – The Wisdom of the Pharaohs, Timothy Freke and Peter Gandy (Piatkus, 1997)

Hindu Scriptures, trans. Nicol Macnicol (J.M. Dent, 1938)

Holy Sutra for Spiritual Healing, Masaharu Taniguchi (Seicho-No-le Truth of Life Movement, North American Missionary Hq., 1981)

Holy Sutra Nectarean Shower of Holy Doctrines, Masaharu Taniguchi (Seicho-No-le Truth of Life Movement, North American Missionary Hq., 1981)

Hymns from the Vedas, ed. Abinash Chandra Bose (Asia Publishing House, 1966)

Islam: Muhammad and his Religion, ed. A. Jeffrey (Liberal Arts Press, 1958)

Khuddaka Patha, trans. Bhikkhu Nanamoli (Pali Text Society, 1960)

Kularnava Tantra, trans. M.P. Pandit (Motilal Barnarsidass, 1965)

Lieh Tzu, trans. L. Giles (Wisdom of the East, 1912)

Living Christianity, Martin Palmer (Element Books, 1993)

Mantramanjari: The Vedic Experience, ed. Raimundo Panikkar (University of California Press, 1977)

Mencius, trans. D.C. Lau (Penguin Books, 1979)

Minor Anthologies of the Pali Canon, trans. F.L. Woodward (Pali Text Society, 1948)

Muhammad and His Religion, trans. Arthur Jeffrey (Liberal Arts Press, 1958)

Muhammad and the Islamic Tradition, trans. Emile Dermenghem/J.M. Watt (Greenwood Press, 1974)

Muntu: An Outline of the New African Culture, Janheinz Jahn (Grove Press, 1961)

Nagarjuna, The Precious Garland and the Song of the Four Mindfulnesses, trans. J. Hopkins and L. Rimpoche (George Allen and Unwin, 1975)

Nahjul Balagha of Hazrat Ali, trans. Syed Mohammed Askari Jafrey (Seerat-Uz-Zahra Committee, 1965)

Nupe Religion, S.F. Nadel (Routledge and Kegan Paul, 1954)

Ofudesaki: The Tip of the Divine Writing Brush, Miki Nakayama (The Headquarters of Tenrikyo Church, 1971)

Our Masters Taught: Rabbinic Stories and Sayings, Jacob J. Petuchowski (Crossroad, 1982)

Pancastikaya of Kundakunda, trans. A. Chakravarti (Bharatiya Jnanapeeth, 1944)

Plato: The Collected Dialogues, ed. Hamilton and Cairns (Bollingen Series LXXI, 1961)

Prayers of the Cosmos, Neil Douglas-Klotz (HarperSanFrancisco, 1994)

Pseudo-Dionysius, trans. Colm Luibheid (Paulist Press, 1987)

Rabbinic Anthology, eds. C.G. Montefiore and H. Loewe (Schocken Books, 1974)

Readings from World Religions, Selwyn Gurney Champion and Dorothy Sort (Watts and Co., 1951)

Reality, trans. S.A. Jain (Vira Shasan Sangha, 1960)

Religion and Society at Cross-roads, Shivamurthy Shivacharya Mahaswamiji (Sri Taralabalu Jagadguru Brihanmath, 1990)

Religion of the Hindus, ed. Kenneth W. Morgan (Ronald Press, 1953)

Sacred Books of the East, many volumes (Clarendon Press, 1884-95)

Sacred Books of the Hindus, ed. B.D. Basu (AMS Press, 1974)

Sacred Texts of the World, ed. Ninian Smart and Richard D. Hecht (Crossroads, 1982)

Sayings of the Fathers, ed. Joseph J. Hertz (Behrman House)

Sayings of Muhammad, trans. Ghazi Ahmad (Sh. Muhammad Ashraf, 1968)

Shinto: The Way of the Gods, W.G. Ashton (Longmans, Green and Co., 1905)

Shramana Mahavira, trans. Sri Dineshandra Sharma (Mitra Parishad, 1976)

Songs of Zarathustra, trans. Dastur Framroze Ardeshir Bode and Piloo Nanavutty (George Allen and Unwin Ltd., 1952)

Sources of the Chinese Tradition, Theodore de Bary (Columbia University Press, 1960)

Sources of Indian Tradition, Theodore de Bary (Columbia University Press, 1958)

Sources of the Japanese Tradition, Theodore de Bary (Columbia University Press, 1958)

Sri Guru Granath Sahib, trans. Gurbachan Singh Talib (Publication Bureau of Punjabi University)

Srimad Bhagavatam, ed. Swami Prabhavananda (Vedanta Press, 1943)

Tao Te Ching, Timothy Freke (Piatkus, 1995)

The Analects of Confucius, trans. Arthur Waley (UK George Allen and Unwin, USA Random House, 1938)

The Art and Thought of Heraclitus, Charles H. Kahn (Cambridge University Press, 1979)

The Autobiography of a Winnebago Indian, Paul Radin (Dover, 1920)

The Babylonian Talmud, trans I. Epstein (Soncino Press, 1948)

The Bhagavad Gita, trans Eknath Easwaran (Arkana, 1985)

The Bhagavadgita, ed. Kees W. Bolle (University of California Press, 1979)

The Chinese Classics, trans. James Legge (Clarendon Press, 1895)

The Complete Guide to World Mysticism, Timothy Freke and Peter Gandy (Piatkus, 1997)

The Crest Jewel of Wisdom and Atma Bodhi by Sankara, trans. Charles Johnston (Llanerch, 1994)

The Diamond Sutra, trans A.F. Price (Shambhala, 1969)

The Dhammapada, trans. Juan Mascar (Penguin Books, 1973)

The Dhammapada, ed. Radhakrishnan (Oxford University Press, 1950)

The Dhammapada, trans. Narada Maha Thera (Vajirama, 1972)

The Dhammapada, trans. Thomas Byrom (Wildwood House, 1976)

The Edicts of Asoka, trans. N.A. Vicam and Richard McKeon (University of Chicago Press, 1959)

The Encyclopaedia of Jewish Concepts, ed. Philip Burnbaum (Hebrew Publishing Co., 1964)

The Ethics of the Talmud: Sayings of the Fathers, ed. R. Travers Herford (Schocken Books, 1925)

The Flower Ornament Scripture: A Translation of the Avatamsaka Sutra, 3 vols., Thomas F. Cleary (Shambhala, 1984-7)

The Forty Traditions of An-Nawawi in The Moslem World 29 no. 2 (Hartford Seminary Foundation, 1938)

The Garuda Purana, ed. Manmatha Natha Dutt (Society for the Resuscitation of Indian Literature, 1908)

The Gospel of Peace of Jesus Christ, trans. Edmond Székely and Purcell Weaver (C.W. Daniel Company Ltd, 1937)

The Group of Discourses, trans. K.R. Norman (Pali Text Society, 1984)

The Hako, a Pawnee Ceremony, Alice C. Fletcher (Twenty-second Annual Report, part 2, Bureau of American Ethnology, 1904)

The Hidden Words of Baha'u'llah (National Spiritual Assembly of the Baha'is of the United States, 1985)

The Holy Bible Revised Standard Version (The Division of Christian Education of the National Council of Churches in the USA, 1971)

The Holy Teachings of Vimalakirti, trans. Robert A.F. Thurman (The Pennsylvania State University Press, 1976)

The Hymns of Zarathustra, trans. Mrs M. Henning (John Murray, 1963)

The I Ching, trans. Richard Wilhelm/C.F. Barnes (Princeton University Press, 1977)

The King James Bible

The Koran, trans. N.J. Dawood (The Penguin Classics, 1956)

The Koran Interpreted, trans. Arthur J. Arberry (Macmillan, 1955)

The Large Sutra on Perfect Wisdom, trans. Edward Conze (University of California Press, 1975)

The Living Talmud: The Wisdom of the Fathers, trans. Judah Goldin (New American Library, 1957)

The Mahaparinirvana Sutra, trans. Kosho Yamamoto (Karinbunko, 1973-75)

The Meaning of the Glorious Qur'an, trans. A Yusef Ali (Dar Al-Kitab Al-Masri, 1938)

The Meaning of the Glorious Qur'an, trans. Muhammad Marmaduke Pickthall (Muslim World League, 1977)

The Messsage of Sikhism, Harbans Singh (Delhi Sikhi Management Committee, 1978)

The Nag Hammadi Library, ed. James M. Robinson (HarperSanFrancisco, 1978)

The New Religions of Japan, H. Thomsen (Charles E. Tuttle Co., 1963)

The New Testament in Modern Translation, trans. J.B. Phillips (Collins, 1960)

The Other Bible, ed. Willis Barnstone (HarperSanFrancisco, 1984)

The Perfection of Wisdom in Eight Thousand Lines and Its Verse Summary, trans. Edward Conze (Four Seasons Foundation, 1983)

The Ramayana of Valmiki, trans. Hari Prasad Shastri (Shanti Sadan, 1962)

The Scripture of the Dead Sea Scrolls, trans Theodor H. Gaster (Secker and Warburg, 1957)

The Seven valleys and the Four Valleys Baha'u'llah (National Spiritual Assembly of the Baha'is of the United States, 1941)

The Song of Songs, Marcia Falk (HarperSanFrancisco, 1990)

The Spiritual Heritage of India, trans. Swami Prabhavananda (Vedanta Press, 1963)

The Spiritual Heritage of India, ed. Swami Prabhavananda (Vedanta Press, 1963)

The Sutra of Hui Neng, trans. Wong Mou-lam (Shambhala, 1969)

The Sutta-Nipata, trans. H. Saddhatissa (Curzon Press, 1985)

The Symposium by Plato, trans. W. Hamilton (The Penguin Classics, 1951)

The Talmudic Anthology, ed. Louis I. Newman (Behrman House, Inc. Publishers, 1945)

The Teachings of the Buddha (Bukkyo Dendo Kyokai, 1984)

The Teachings of the Magi, trans. R.C. Zaehner (London, 1956)

The Tibetan Book of the Dead, trans. W.Y. Evans-Wentz (Oxford University Press, 1960)

The Two Buddhist Books in Mahayana, trans. Upansika Chihmann (Rumford, 1936)

The Upanishads, trans. Eknath Easwaran (Nilgiri Press, 1985)

The Upanishads, trans. Juan Mascar (Penguin Books, 1967)

The Wisdom of Confucius, trans. Lin Yutang (Random House, 1938)

The Zohar, trans Harry Sperling and Maurice Simon (Soncno Press, 1934)

Tibet's Great Yogi Milarepa, trans. Lama Kali Dawa-Samdup (Oxford University Press, 1928)

Timaeus by Plato, trans Desmond Lee (Penguin Classics, 1965)

Traditions of the Prophet, comp. Javad Nurbakhsh (Khaniqahi-Nimatullahi Publications, 1981)

Treasury of Jewish Quotations, ed. Joseph L. Baron (Jason Aronston, 1985)

Treasury of Mahayana Sutras, trans. Garma C.C. Chang (The Pennsylvania University Press, 1983)

What the Buddha Taught, ed. Walpola Rahula (Grove Press, 1974)

World Scripture, ed. Andrew Wilson (Paragon House, 1991)

Yin Chih Wen: The Tract of the Quiet Way, trans. D.T. Suzuki and Paul Carus (Open Court Publishing Co., 1906)

Yoruba Oral Tradition, ed. Wande Abimbola (Ibadan University Press Ltd., 1975)

Note: Many of the quotations in this book have been edited or rendered into contemporary English by Timothy Freke, often based on a number of different translations.

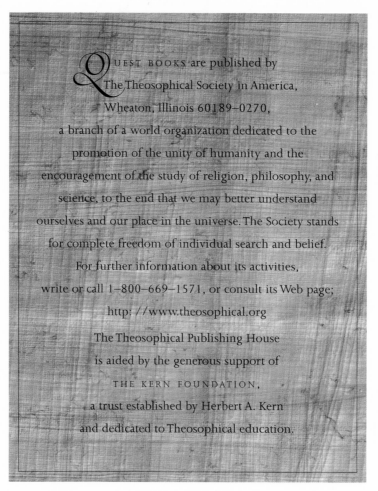

QUEST BOOKS are published by
The Theosophical Society in America,
Wheaton, Illinois 60189–0270,
a branch of a world organization dedicated to the
promotion of the unity of humanity and the
encouragement of the study of religion, philosophy, and
science, to the end that we may better understand
ourselves and our place in the universe. The Society stands
for complete freedom of individual search and belief.
For further information about its activities,
write or call 1–800–669–1571, or consult its Web page;
http://www.theosophical.org

The Theosophical Publishing House
is aided by the generous support of
THE KERN FOUNDATION,
a trust established by Herbert A. Kern
and dedicated to Theosophical education.